THE UNVEILING

"PAIN, TRAUMA, & TRUTH"

MONICA WILLIAMS

Hardcover ISBN: 978-1-63616-005-4
eBook ISBN: 978-1-63616-007-8
Audiobook ISBN: 978-1-63616-006-1

Published By Opportune Independent Publishing Co.
www. opportunepublishing.com

Printed in the United States of America
For permission requests, email the author with the subject line as "Attention: Permissions Coordinator" to the email address below:
monica.williams0313@gmail.com

WARNING:
There is sensitive content involving child sexual abuse in this book. It contains graphic descriptions and may be confronting and disturbing.

If you or anyone you know is currently, or has been, abused and needs help please contact the Darkness to Light Child Sexual Abuse at 1-866-367-5444 or the Rape, Abuse, and Incest National Network (RAINN) at 1-800-656-4673, Or, contact them by going to www.rainn.org
You are not alone.

TABLE OF CONTENTS

DEDICATION

I would like to take this time to recognize every person who has gone through any childhood pain, trauma, rape, or molestation.

This book is dedicated to you and I hope one day you'll share that story of hurt and triumph.

If you still find yourself drowning in the past or feeling alone, there is hope. No matter how many times you get knocked down, get back up and never stop fighting. Courage is not about who can, it is about who will rise up, stand firm, and take their place by telling their unadulterated truth.

Remember, you are an overcomer and you will survive… because I did. Your truth will set you and others free.

ᴛʜᴇUNVEILING

ACKNOWLEDGMENTS

I would like to thank my spouse, children, family and friends for believing in me through this journey. Thank you all for your support, motivation, and encouragement while sharing my life story and experiences as I lived it.

Also, thank you to every trauma survivor that has shared your truth to help me and others.

THE UNVEILING

INTRODUCTION

Writing my story gives a voice to countless voiceless men and women who have had their innocence taken away and have been violated as a child and out of the fear of rejection have never spoken about it. After being invited into my world of child sexual abuse, trauma, failed relationships, and much more you will develop a greater understanding of the experiences that have shaped my life. Writing this book was one of the most difficult and challenging things I've had to do in my life. Me publicly exposing my past for the first time placed me in a vulnerable, yet liberating, place of power. Having gone through the worst betrayal one could ever experience changed me in unimaginable ways. Truths that have never been revealed can cause you to relive the devastation of your trauma in many subtle ways. Writing those once buried secrets on paper, and sharing my life as I lived and experienced it was as honest and accurate as the pain itself. *The Unveiling* represents my coming from behind what has been secretly covered up for so long. I hope sharing my story will inspire many others to do the same.

My goal is for this book to bring some much-needed healing of the soul, restoration of the mind, and reconciliation with self. Release yourself of your unspoken truths so that you can be free to live the rest of your life in peace.

It was never your fault.

™UNVEILING

CHAPTER 1

ONCE UPON A TIME

(In the Beginning with My Grandmother)

"Parent-child relationships are complex. Grandmother-grandchild relationships are simple. Grandmas are short on criticism and long on love."
—Janet Lanese

I was born Monica Renee Richardson on March 13, 1972, to first-time parents, Jeanette Wilkins and Dock Richardson. That's when it all began. I was released into a world to be cared for by two imperfect people who I would one day call, mommy and daddy. Parents are there to love, nurture, and take care of us in ways no one else can. I was in total dependence of my mother, counting on her to meet all my needs, as newborns usually are. My mom lived in a home with my grandmother and uncle on the east side of the city. She was young, beautiful, fun, loving, and full of life to live… definitely not ready to have a kid. Imagine her surprise when she found herself pregnant with me.

I wonder what my dad and grandmother's response was. She was 17 years old and my dad was 21 when she gave birth to me. She was inexperienced and clueless as to what a baby would need besides the obvious. My mother was two months away from turning 18 and probably thought she would finish high school unscathed. However, being responsible for a baby changed that, so she did not return back to school. By then, my father had learned how to navigate his way through life and with my mom. Like most teen pregnancies, I'm sure I was unplanned and an unexpected surprise. In fact, I'm certain my conception was a mistake that happened while she was enjoying a night of fun with my dad.

What am I going to do with a baby? Was probably the thought racing through her mind. I can only imagine what my mother must have felt carrying me for nine months knowing the day of my birth was approaching and her life would change forever. She could have aborted or given me away being so young, but she didn't.

I wondered if it was love at first sight when she held me in her arms, kissed my forehead, placed my tiny little hand in her hand, and stared down into my eyes.

I'm sure the reality of taking care of a newborn was frightening; maybe she felt alone and scared. However, she summoned up enough courage to give birth to two more children later on while still living with my grandmother. Unfortunately, my father was not as present to assist my mother or grandmother with taking care of us.

My grandmother played a major role in raising me, and for the early part of my childhood, she was my primary caregiver. The time I spent with her made me very close with her. My mother was gone a lot, partying and hanging out in the streets. I cannot imagine how that must have made my grandmother feel.

There were three of us who my grandmother was responsible for taking care of while wondering where her daughter was for days at a time. I'm sure my mother knew we were in good hands, which made it easier for her to stay out as often and for as long as she did, away from her responsibilities.

My grandmother was not in the best of health and I still cannot understand how she managed to take care of three children with very little help and means. She knew how to make something out of nothing. She always prepared meals that were filling and satisfying to our bellies; we definitely didn't go hungry.

Although I was very young, my grandmother filled the emotional absence of my mother while I was growing up. Not only did I love my grandmother, I was attached to her, but I still wanted my mother all of the time. I'm sure there were moments when my grandmother felt more like a mother to me, as she was fulfilling both roles. As a result of my mother having me so young, my grandmother did more than play a part in my upbringing; she was mostly responsible for raising me. Of course, I did not understand the difference, because we lived in the house with my grandmother. I was a young child, and not only did I need my mother, but my father too. She did not talk about the times when my mother was not home; these were just normal days for my grandmother. Honestly, I didn't know that the time spent with my grandmother was anything out of the ordinary.

In addition to my grandmother taking care of us, she also watched my cousins while my aunt worked. My cousins and I were very close, more like siblings and friends than first cousins. They were a few years older, but we had a lot of fun together playing games in and outdoors at grandma's house. We were a part of each other's daily lives growing up and enjoyed being together. The hardest part was always when it was time for our cousins to go home. We didn't want the fun to end.

The Lens of a Child

One can only assume that parents do their best to protect and shield their children from negativity as much as possible. We knew, as children, there was a place that we stayed in, and it was called "a child's place," as we heard, "Stay in a child's place," so many times. In a child's place, we were not allowed to question adults, or be in their conversations or business. We did whatever we were told to do, without any complaining or back talk. When our grandmother, mother, aunt or any adult called our name, we answered, "Yes, ma'am" or "Yes, sir", out of pure respect for our elders. It was a way of acknowledging our place within the setting and respecting theirs.

When my mom and dad met back in the day, I imagined having a baby was not at the top of their to-do list. The pleasures of unknowingly making me was exciting—but how serious were they both about actually taking care of me? One thing is for certain: They were not ready for the responsibility of being parents to me and my brother, which forced my grandmother into the parental role. Kids do not ask to be born, and surely, it's not up to them how they're raised by the two people who chose to create them.

In 1972, my parents were young and still all about their own pleasures and desires when I was born. My only brother, with whom I share both parents, was born the following year, and my sister was born three years later. From what I can remember, there was a man who would visit my mom on occasions… as I know now, he was my sister's father.

My grandmother, Anna, raised us until she fell ill and passed away on February 8, 1978, I was one month away from turning six years old. I did not have a lot of years with her, but my time with her was unforgettable. I paid close attention to her as she provided a stabled, safe, and loving environment for us. She had a calming presence about her and patience that filled a room with peace. There was something special about my grandmother that would make you feel like everything was going to be alright. She made my life simple and fun, I was proud to be her granddaughter.

During those fun, "good ol' days" some of my childhood memories were when I played with baby dolls, had conversations with imaginary friends, and often spent time playing silly games (hide-and-seek, duck-duck-goose, ring around the rosie) with my brother and cousins. My sister was too young to actually play along, but she was there with us.

The three-bedroom house in the city was full of our grandmother's love and a lot of interesting stories. How can I forget the wringer washing machine near the kitchen when my uncle's arm was caught in the wringer, and the olive oil that Grandma used to bless and heal us with? There was also a monster that we used to see at the foot of the bed... well, at least we believed we did. Lastly, who could forget the mud pies we made out of dirt in the backyard?

When I was five years old, I was playing in my uncle's work boots when I fell down the steps in the backyard and split my forehead open. Unfortunately, my mother was not home at the time and, in a panic, my grandmother called my aunt. She rushed over and drove me to the hospital, where I received several stitches. I remember it so vividly—the pain was so excruciating that it took a couple of doctors and my aunt to hold me down because I was afraid of the needle used to numb around the gash on my forehead.

As a little girl, I was left wondering, *Where is my mommy?* While the tears were rolling down my face, I was calling and yelling for her repeatedly. Perhaps I thought the pain would have been less severe had she been by my side. That was the very first time I felt real pain, and I had to suffer through it without my mother. Even today, the scar on my forehead reminds me of that dreadful day and of her absence during a time when I needed her the most.

While I was in capable hands, there was no better place to be than in the arms of my mother. I cannot remember if she came home that night or a day or two later. One thing that is for certain is that she was not at the hospital to calm my fears and wipe my tears. When I think about it now, as I was too young then, but my grandmother was probably impacted by what happened to me the most. She probably blamed herself for not keeping a closer eye on me, but it was not her fault. I assume she was doing the best that she could. With all things considered, she did have her own health challenges she was dealing with.

My grandmother's health was failing and she had been in and out of the hospital. I knew she wasn't feeling well often, but she kept pushing. She was a diabetic, but that did not stop her from spending quality time with us and being our babysitter until the disease took a toll on her body. I wished my grandmother did not get sick and could have lived a healthier life. Despite her aches and pains, she did her very best to not allow it to get in the way of taking care of her family. She stepped in and was very present in my life until the day she died. Some days were better than others, but she took great pleasure in taking care of me and my siblings.

Grandma Anna was a God-fearing Christian woman who took us to church often. She was small in stature, standing at just five feet, three inches tall, but that was no measure of her strength. She was sweet and loving, but quick and accurate with the belt. When she said not to do something, that's exactly what she meant, and she did not play around.

I recall a time when she gave instructions for the grandchildren to stay in the backyard while playing. Well, my cousins decided to walk to the corner store; of course, my brother and I tagged along. Eventually, when my grandmother came to the back door, she did not see us playing in the yard. Back in those days, there was no such thing as child abuse when it came to disciplining your children. While standing in front of the corner store, I distinctly remember hearing Grandma Anna yelling, "Didn't I tell y'all not to leave from out of that backyard?"

She beat us with her belt all the way back home, which was just a short distance, but felt like miles away. The corner store could literally be seen from our backyard, but that whooping made the distance seem much further. Once back at home, she finished spanking our behinds, then we all had to line up for prayer with that good ol' "Blessed Olive Oil" she rubbed on our foreheads... I guess to rid us of our rebellion. Afterwards, we had the talk about following directions and the consequences of not listening, as if the belt was not enough. My grandmother had her hands full raising us, but I am glad we had her to depend on. She was probably used to doing what she had to do, because if she didn't do it, who would have?

We did not grow up privileged or with silver spoons in our mouths. Grandma Anna used to make us peanut butter and jelly sandwiches that I did not like, but ate anyway. Back then, we were not given options of what to eat; whatever was placed in front of you on your plate was what you ate. They did not ask our opinions, so we knew better than to say, "I do not like…" or "I do not want a peanut butter and jelly sandwich."

To this day, I still do not like peanut butter.

Grandma Anna knew how to make a meal out of what she randomly had, always making sure there was enough food to go around. My family and I had what we needed: We ate every day and had a house to live in, clothes on our backs and shoes on our feet. My grandmother grew up in a generation where money was tight and food was scarce; therefore, she made do with what she had. Surely, there were times we were barely making it financially, but my grandmother made sure nothing was wasted, especially food.

Telling stories, laughing, playing games, and sitting quietly during a thunderstorm were teachable and memorable moments. For example, our grandmother would have us sit still with the lights off in a corner while it was thunder and lightning. Bathing was absolutely forbidden during this time as well. Maybe she thought we would get struck by lightning while naked. Whatever her reasoning, we were not getting in her bathtub during a storm and we had to stay away from windows! Grandma Anna had a home remedy for every situation, problem, and sickness. I wish she would have healed herself from being a diabetic. The absence of my mother had grown familiar while the presence of my grandmother remained comforting and consistent. If only it was enough that my mother was hardly ever around… where was my dad? I do not recall seeing him at all around this part of my life, but I know my mother was "running the streets" with him when he was close to the area where we lived.

He saw us when we were born and probably a few times in between, but I had no memory of him or any time he spent with us that I could recall. I later found out my grandmother was not that fond of my dad, and at some point, he was not allowed in her home. No matter what, it did not stop my mother from being with him whenever she had the opportunity to.

I had gotten used to being with my grandmother and seeing my mother in phases after being gone for many days. I never knew the actual length of time she was not at home, but I did know when I was not seeing her. I always felt my grandmother would never leave me—in fact, I never wanted to leave her either. I remember the softness of her voice and the warmth of her hands holding mine while I sat next to her one evening as she told me a random story. There was something mesmerizing about Grandma Anna that night, more than her presence and words. If only I could have understood the story she was telling me and why as I looked up at her face and thought, *I love you, Grandma.*

Mixed Emotions

My grandmother continued to get sick and was eventually hospitalized, but that time, she never went back home. One minute, she was there, and the next, she was gone. She was an insulin-dependent Type 1 diabetic with some amputations that she never fully recovered from. I am not sure how long she was in the hospital, but it seemed like forever. I had hoped we'd get another chance to spend more time with her. My grandmother always provided reassurance and I knew I could depend on her to be there… until she was not.

One evening, my mother had to break the unfortunate news to us about Grandma Anna's passing. I was too young and did not necessarily understand what was going on, but I did know we were not going to see her ever again. I was overwhelmed with crying and sadness, but my mom didn't allow us to attend the funeral. I was not prepared to lose my grandmother and wished I could have seen her one last time to say goodbye. I'm assuming my mother wanted us to remember our grandmother how we saw her last. This was our first encounter with death and I realized she had been taken away from us and wouldn't be around to squeeze me tight and give me hugs. My grandmother died and I didn't know how to feel or if the tears would ever go away. What would my life be like without her, she was my security blanket?

Grandma Anna was described as a woman of strength, forgiveness, peace, and kindness, and the glue holding the family together with love. She was a bright, shining light that I wish never went out. In the few short years I had with her, she made me feel loved and secured. Immediately after her passing, I wanted her back in my life. The house was empty without her in it and it didn't feel the same. My cousins and brother all were just as down in the dumps over losing Grandma; however, I took it as losing a grandmother and a second mother. My mother, aunt and uncle lost a parent, and I'm sure their grief was heavy as well. Why did she have to die and leave us all alone? She was very special to a lot of people.
I was unable to share my grief; it was hard to register my feelings, as it was my first experience with the death of a loved one. Grandma Anna always gave us comfort, but then we were left to comfort one another. Although my mother worried my grandmother a lot, I know she was hurt deeply and in pain over losing her mother. We all wished we had more time, as the time we had together with her was not enough. It seemed like it all happened so suddenly—she was gone and life was different.

Life Without Grandma

Shortly after the death of my grandmother, we had to move.

I did not know anything about my father's side of the family, but obviously, my mother was very familiar with them in order for them to let us live there. We moved in with my paternal aunt and her husband, who lived on the west side of town. They welcomed us with open arms once we arrived, but I didn't know them; they were strangers. But we quickly learned to adapt, as we had no other choice.

My aunt would often tell me and my brother how much we looked like our dad. She shared stories about him as a young boy and all the crazy and fun things he did that made him light up a room like a movie star. I marveled at the stories she told of him and hoped that I would one day know him for myself. I wished I knew where he was. Nobody really kept in touch with my father on a consistent basis because he was all over the place, but they knew he was somewhere in Virginia and would be calling soon. He was known for disappearing and then randomly reappearing; those were the times my mother would spend with him. She didn't see much of my father after the death of my grandmother; it was like he had vanished into thin air. My aunt was overly nice to us, and besides talking about my father, she enjoyed fixing delicious home-cooked meals. She reminded me a little of my grandmother.

My aunt had a grapevine tree in her backyard from which she and my uncle made wine and grape jelly. My brother and I would watch some days as they smashed the grapes. Despite the exciting new experience of living with my aunt and uncle, I could not help but think about if I would ever see my father, the "movie star." I went to bed many nights hoping that he would show up the next day. My mother had lost contact with him and wondered when she would see him again too. In the meantime, I just enjoyed spending time with my family and getting to know them.

Living there gave me an opportunity to meet some cousins my age who would often visit. There were a lot of aunts and uncles who had children; it was never a dull moment. When they would stay over, they would scare me and my brother at night telling spooky stories in the dark and playing scary games. We would be so afraid that we couldn't go to sleep with the lights off. Those times were fun! No matter how scared we were, we did what silly little kids do—play.

Although the death of Grandma Anna was devastating, living with my aunt and uncle brought my mom closer to us. It was like a new beginning. She became more present and available, and we loved spending more time with her. My mother got us ready for school in the mornings and picked us up from school in the afternoons. Seeing her in the mother role put a smile on my face. She was taking care of us and we got to see her all of the time. Things were definitely changing. When she would go out to visit our other family members, she would take us along now. This was different because she used to leave us with Grandma Anna and we would not see or hear from her for days at a time. Although I didn't quite understand death and grief, I knew I wanted my mother close, more than ever before, so I could feel comforted and supported.

Meanwhile, my aunt started to get noticeably ill. She became extremely weak, sleeping a lot and eating less, and my uncle had to care for her on a more consistent basis. She was not the same woman I met when she welcomed us into her home. She began to wear wigs and soon after started wearing scarves to cover her bald head. Due to her progressive illness, we found ourselves having to move again. Shortly thereafter, we were told my aunt had passed away from cancer, an illness I was too young to know about. I do not remember it ever being explained to me. Once again, someone whom I loved and cared about was gone. I was only seven years old and had already experienced two great losses in my life, and it was confusing to me. I felt an unexplainable, yet familiar, sadness upon me. I thought about my Grandma Anna and how much I loved and missed her. Now I had to think of my aunt in the same way. Dealing with the death of loved ones seemed to be one of the hardest things I ever had to do as a young girl.

Me at 5 years old.

My beloved Grandma Anna.

My first cousins.

My one and only brother.

My uncle whose work boots I fell down the steps in.

CHAPTER 2

SECRETS IN THE CLOSET

(Nightmares Everywhere)

***This troubling and unknown world would one day
become familiar to the eyes of the innocent in a way that
would change her life forever.***
—Monica Williams

As a young kid, I was left to cope with the loss of my loving grandmother and my precious aunt. I was lucky enough to have them both in my life although not for very long. As a result, I was more quiet and withdrawn, not knowing how to talk about their death. When you are a child it's more difficult to express the things you don't understand. I was scared and nothing around me felt real anymore. I wasn't sure if someone else I loved was going to die and leave me. I didn't know how to handle the loss, especially of my grandmother and I had to process those feelings around family members I hardly knew, but had seen at church when Grandma Anna took us along with her.

Once we moved in with them, I noticed my mother started leaving us again like she did when we lived with my grandmother. She did not leave us alone but with the relatives who seemed ok with watching us.

I was still full of sadness and was left in an apartment with people I don't think understood the emptiness I felt in my life. Being a child, I tried to make the best out of another living situation, honestly I didn't know what else to do. I thought if I reminisce more about my grandmother that would fill the voids of sadness. I wanted to not feel the grief of the loss and questioned why she had to die.

Although, we had another place to stay I wished we had a house of our own. These family members were not strangers, I just did not know them as well as they knew me. In a corner off to myself, I would day dream about the life I had with my grandmother, I was missing her. But all of a sudden, once the daydreaming was over, my surroundings felt strange and I sensed feelings of disappointment. At the age of 7, I remember thinking, *I don't like it here, I did not feel comfortable.*

I had been enjoying my childhood up to that point and then everything changed. I found myself looking after my siblings, something I didn't do before. When my mother left the house she would tell me to keep an eye on them although other adults were home. I don't know why I felt the safest while dreaming, maybe I wanted to disconnect from my reality. I knew for sure something was uncomfortable in the space I was in, it could have been me really missing my grandmother and aunt.

Being a kid was not the same anymore and my mother started hanging out again so she was not there to help me figure out my feelings. I was 7 years old and something was off. It had to be the grief, but it felt awkward in the apartment with my family. I was happy that we did have a place to stay, but we didn't have privacy. We were cramped in an apartment with three other people. I wondered when we initially moved in where we were going to sleep because all of the rooms were occupied. At least at my aunt's house, my siblings and I shared a room with a bed to sleep in. My mother was thankful we had somewhere else to stay temporarily, even if that meant we'd sleep on the floor.

As the oldest child, I was always told that I was a pretty little girl that acted more mature than my age. My family would jokingly say, "Look at that little old lady."

Most of my family had weird nicknames so mine became, "Little old lady. "It was not out of the ordinary to be called something other than your real name. Not sure why that name sounded funny, but we'd all laugh about it.

Not long after staying with my relatives, one of my male family members who was in his late 20s or early 30s, a churchgoing man—one would say a "Christian"—kissed me on the lips. No one had ever kissed me like that before. It was so odd to me that I told my mother and she said, "Oh that›s how he is. He always kisses people to show love, he didn't mean any harm."

What did I know? I was only a child and did not quite understand what it all meant, but I believed my mother; maybe it was innocent. I also wanted to believe he meant no harm, but I felt weird around him afterward. I was not able to explain it, but I knew something felt wrong. I was right because he kissed me again, but I didn't tell my mother that time, like she said he was "showing me love." I told myself *maybe adults kiss kids on the lips.*

When my mother would leave, I never wanted to stay behind, but she didn't always take me along. I did not feel comfortable by myself and wanted my mother near my side but that didn't happen as often as I would have liked it to. Who could I tell about the other kiss and would they believe me? I did not know what to do, but I definitely was afraid of him. I was scared to be in the same room as him—even with people around, I was uncomfortable with the way he made me feel and how he would look at me.

More time passed and things only escalated.

He started to get even more inappropriate during the times when my siblings and I were left home alone with him. He would call me into his room and put his hand down my pants and touch my private area. I didn't know if I was supposed to be letting him do it or not; he was family so I trusted him. I assumed it was another way he showed his love, like the kiss.

As a child, I was so confused about everything that was going on how was I supposed to understand any of it? I tried to make myself believe it wasn't happening by not talking about it and keeping my feelings bottled up inside. I couldn't tell anyone; I was afraid they wouldn't believe or listen to me anyways. I wish what I was going through was only in my head! But it was not! It was as real as my name. I was not familiar with being touched in that way... no little girl should be. I felt even less safe around him and I was becoming a frightened child in his presence, which somehow went unnoticed by everyone else. I hoped at least my mother would see something was different about the way I responded when she left me behind. All I wanted was for her to not leave or to take me with her. I had words deep down that she could not hear; I wanted to tell her, but I didn't know how to.

One Saturday morning, I was playing outside and I had to use the bathroom, but I was too scared to go into the house because no one was home except for him. I could not hold it any longer, so I went inside and there he was signaling me to come to his room. It was as if he were watching me on the outside and waiting for me to come into the house. I did not know what to expect, but I knew it was not good—it never was.

As I came from the bathroom he was still waiting at his door, so I went into his room. He told me it was our secret and not to tell anyone, and I agreed. He laid me on his bed and pulled down my panties. I did not want him to hurt me, but he did. I was frightened as he undid his pants and looked me in my eyes as he rubbed his penis on my private area. I was nervous and afraid as he continued rubbing it faster and faster and then he stopped. What had just happened to me was unexplainable to say the least. I did not know if he was fearful of someone walking in and catching him or not, but I had hoped someone did. Maybe that explains why he kept the door open—to hear if someone came into the house. After he was done, he pulled my bottoms up and reminded me of our secret. *How was it my secret too?* I thought.

I did not know how to feel afterward. I wanted to avoid him, but I could not; I saw him at home every day. I had gone from living with my grandmother and my aunt being a little girl, as I should, to this. Never in a child's wildest dreams should this have been going on. I should have been left to dreaming, fairytales and having fun. Instead, everything I thought should be happening to me wasn't.

He was family. I thought I could trust him until he gave me reasons not to. He changed my idea of him by exposing me to that type of inappropriateness. I wondered if I was to blame for what he had done to me. There was something brewing on the inside of me that could not be easily expressed verbally.

Of course, the moments when my mother and other family members were not at the house was when he would do those horrible things to me. I was not sure what attracted him to me; I was a 7 year old little girl, weighing every bit of 50 pounds. I did not know how to make him stop touching me or if I could; he was stronger than I was and much older. It was just so hard for me to believe he could do that to me, I played it over and over in my head.

He was a grown man and should have never engaged himself with me in that way. I thought I had no choice but to let him; it seemed like that's what he wanted me to do, and all I wanted was for someone to save me from him. His presence made me so uneasy, that I wished I had a safer place to hide. Why didn't my mother see I was hurting or that something was wrong? Why couldn't she see it? I wanted to tell her so bad, but it was a secret and I promised to stay quiet. He was a well-known and respected man in the community and church, everybody loved him so no one would've believed me. I felt so alone in my fears.

I knew living there was only temporary, but I wanted to run away immediately. There were many nights that I was too scared to go to sleep hoping he would not somehow find a way to come get me. Every time he walked through the door from work my body tensed up. I felt like a bad little girl, like I was doing something wrong by keeping his dirty secret. I just did not want to be around him anymore!

I wanted to be far away from him so he could never touch me again.

Who would ever believe me, I felt helpless; I was a child, and it would've been his word against mine. I had to carry that secret with me, acting as if nothing were wrong... but everything was. I felt unprotected by my mother, the person who was supposed to protect me. But she could not protect me from what she did not know. I existed in a family that couldn't see or notice that I was silently screaming for their help.

I wanted his touch off of me! What he had done was so wrong and I knew it did not feel right. He violated my innocence and did unspeakable things that he could never take back. I tried to block out what happened, but it wouldn't go away. Was it something I said or did that gave him the impression that I wanted him to do that? I must have invited him somehow, why else would he do it? The thoughts of him touching me were always present, and I felt ashamed and dirty. I blamed myself for what he had done, believing I somehow caused it.

I did only what I was told to do, I never liked him touching me, but I did not want to be in trouble if I refused to let him. I was so scared! What was I supposed to do, besides keep silent? My life was stained with the disgust of his touch. I did not feel the same after that.

The day came that I was hoping for, we had to move again, and I was so happy. I didn't care why or what had happened—I just wanted to leave!

Living in the Trenches

We moved in with another one of our relatives. I was hoping it would be a safer place. Anything would be so much better than the previous apartment we lived in. I did not know what to do or how to act around my family. But I did know that they were not supposed to harm you. That was not true with my family at least. I was fearful and jumpy all of the time, watching, waiting, and expecting for something bad to happen, feelings I never had until a member of my family hurt me. After what I had been through, I was not sure whom I could believe or trust in my life. I had not told anyone and I was having a hard time with my emotions. *What could I have done to stop him*, I thought.? Worrying if it would happen again in the new place. I was looking around at my family and no longer felt safe in the world I was living in.

I wanted to forget what happened, nobody needed to know, I was too afraid and ashamed to talk about what he'd done to me. Silence was better than speaking because it was hard to put into words, I was just a little girl and I didn't want to be seen! I just didn't want to be near my family, especially since I did not trust them.

Toxic Family

We went from one bad situation to another. These relatives did not take long to show their true colors and make us feel unwanted. They were not nice at all toward my siblings and me—when my mother wasn't around, of course. I felt like I was always fighting for something and being scared of everything. My cousins who were within me and my brother's age range, would threaten us not to say anything to our mothers when they would do mean and hateful things to us, mainly the oldest cousin. They did not like us living there and definitely didn't want us around, so they made being there miserable. I did not want to be near these people either, but what choice did I have—*none*.

Their mother was not the nicest person, somewhat hateful actually. My mother would leave us home with them while she was out partying with other family and friends. I'm sure she felt we were safe; I don't believe she would knowingly leave us in a bad situation. She was unaware of how we were being treated and when she returned home, we acted as if everything was okay because we were too afraid to say anything. When my mother was told how we were acting it was explained in a way as though we did something wrong and had to be spanked. We were always being disciplined for being "bad," even though we weren't doing anything wrong. How could I tell my mother that they were not telling the truth, without getting in more trouble? I hated it there!

One evening, during dinner, my oldest cousin took my sister's food from her and dared us to tell; he just loved taunting us for no reason. It was always something going on that I had to protect us from. I tried to keep us all together in one area so we wouldn't be accused of things, but it was difficult to manage by myself. They made life harder for no reason and we were forced into the situation. I had no control over what they would do, but I was always nervous because they were constantly doing things to us..

One day, my cousin tried to force my little sister to eat food from the trash can... he definitely was not fond of her. I had to stop him, so I hit him with a broomstick, which made him angry. He chased after me until his younger sibling stopped him. He was so intimidating, like a bully. I did not like him very much and he was another person I didn't want in my life. I was unsure of what type of family I had, but it was troubling and kept me in a panic.

Life didn't seem fair, but I had no voice to speak up; I was always afraid of what or how to say something, scared to be called a liar. With my mother being gone all of the time, which was not unusual, we were left to defend ourselves. We needed her! Why did they hate us so much? What were we doing so wrong to be treated the way we were by them? We tried to tell our mother we didn't like it there, but she didn't see anything wrong and we didn't know how to explain why we wanted to move. The nights our mother was not home, I kept my siblings as close to me as I possibly could to keep us out of harm's way.

Life as a child was no longer simple; I had become more afraid of the people I was forced to be around. Imagine everyday living in fear and always waiting for the next bad thing to happen. The problem was that I felt like I didn't belong with my family, but I had nowhere else to go. I had absolutely no control over my dysfunctional environment. Enjoying my childhood was a big missing piece of my life. As a young girl, my feelings were all over the place, not knowing how to deal with the things that were happening all around me.

My mother was young and loved to party all of the time. She loved us and did her best, I just wished she didn't leave us so much. But she would be home during the week to make sure we went to school and had what we needed. School was a much better place for us; it was a way to get away from it all. We hated the weekends because that's mostly when she'd be gone.

One day, my older cousin took my dollar that I planned to use to get a frozen cup with and he told me not to tell. I told my mother anyway and when she saw him she approached him about it. Of course, he became angry and lied about taking my money. I was in the house while my mother and another relative were sitting on the steps across the street. As I was looking out the window, I saw my older cousin walking toward the house. I was scared and tried to hide under the bed, but he caught me and got in my face, yelling at me. At that time, I was 8 years old and he was 12. He said, "Didn't I tell you not to say anything?"

As I was crying and trembling, he punched me in my mouth and busted my lip. My mother heard the scream from outside of the house because the window was open. You can just imagine the look on her face when she saw me. She asked, "What happened to you?"

While crying, I told her what he had done and she aggressively went after him, placing her hands around his neck and choking him, he could barely breathe. Another relative pulled my mother away from him as she was yelling every curse word she could utter at him. She called him every name but a child of God.

Although I was crying with blood dripping from my mouth and in pain, I was glad my mother was there to finally see the trauma her children had been enduring. I didn't need to try to convince her this time of anything; she witnessed it for herself. After all the stuff we had gone through and the lies, I hoped we'd move after that situation... and we did. There was no way we could have stayed comfortably in that house without further consequences, there was no resolving the situation.

My mother was furious. She was determined we were moving from that house the same day and started packing our clothes immediately. I knew we didn't have a place of our own to move to, I just didn't want to stay with another family member; so far they were not working out. I would have taken getting punched in the mouth a million times if that's what it took to get us out of that very hard and difficult living situation. Sadly, all of these bad, negative experiences gave me much to fear. At the time, I just wondered where we would go to live. We moved around a couple of times after Grandma Anna died, but my mother kept us together. No matter how bad the situation was, she always managed to find a way.

Later that day, my mother's sister came to get us and we moved in temporarily with my mother's brother in his one-bedroom apartment. My uncle was a single man with no children or girlfriend. He did not want us there too long. Besides, there was not enough space for us all.

We lived with him for a short time until one night my siblings and I were left home alone and we almost caught the apartment on fire. My uncle worked the night shift, so he was not able to stay home to watch us the nights my mother was not there. I tried to cook us some food that ended up burning and we threw it into the trash can, which then started a small fire. We put the trash can out on the fire escape and the neighbors called the fire department after smelling smoke.

When they arrived, I opened the door and they noticed we were home alone. The police were called and were about to remove us from the home because no adults were present. We were crying, asking if we could call our stepfather (my sister's dad) because I knew his number by memory. He was called and came to get us to take us to his home. He left a note on the door for my mother telling her where we were and what happened.

When my mother arrived at his home, she was glad we were all safe, but also upset about the entire situation. At this point, my childhood was in a state of constant chaos and I was still struggling with those recent experiences I was not talking about. My mother was to blame for leaving us unattended and needed to take accountability for that part. She was actually mad at me, as if I was the one in the wrong for the police coming to the house. It was too much responsibility for me to handle at such a young age! I don't think she fully understood that she'd left her 8-year-old daughter in an apartment alone to care for a 7- and 4-year-old who happened to get hungry and needed to eat. After she had a long conversation (or shall I say, argument) with my stepdad, we ended up moving in with him for a while. *Here we go again. Moving never felt so exhausting and we were going to our fourth new elementary school within two years.*

Although, I looked innocent and cute, this was the tender sweet age of seven. I was never the same afterward and being a little girl had been smeared. My innocence was lost and took a terrible turn. Why did he have to do this to me?

A terrible turn.

CHAPTER 3

THE WHIRLWIND

(Tumultuous Situations)

Right Place, Right Time. It Was A Whirlwind; It All Just
Happened So Fast.
—Brian McCann

Shortly after we moved in with my stepfather, I assumed he and my mother called themselves being back together as a couple because the next thing I knew, she was pregnant. Although those two were not legally married at the time, he was as close to a dad as I ever had, and I needed that. I always imagined being a family, living in a stable home and possibly feeling safe again, and he provided that for us. I was afraid to get comfortable because I figured it would only be a matter of time before we would be moving again.

My stepdad lived in a nice, quiet neighborhood in Baltimore City on a busy one-way street. Every car that drove by honked their horns while yelling his name. He was a popular man known by everyone. He would wave and have the biggest smile in the world, with a contagious laugh. I admired him because he loved my brother and me as if we were his own children. Although he had another daughter from a previous relationship, it did not interfere with him treating my brother and me like his biological children— referring to us only as his son and daughter!

He was the daddy I hoped for, since mine was missing in action. He was a provider; he took good care of us while we lived with him and he was a great cook. I just needed something solid in my life; I wanted to trust again and I was hoping things would not change. He made sure we had all we needed. He was stern with us, but loving at the same time. We had consistency and stability, it was a real family and I did not want it to end.

Why does everything good seem to always turn bad? One day, I heard my mom and stepdad arguing downstairs and I went to see what was going on. I sat on the steps as I watched the man I thought could do no wrong yell at my mother. I wanted the argument to be over and for them to make up, I was not ready to move again. I never imagined he could get so upset and hoped he'd calm down—especially since she was pregnant with his child. She seemed just as mad and was crying, which made me cry. I could not figure out what caused the disagreement, but I hoped it would never happen again. What were a couple of minutes seemed like hours before it all stopped and he walked away saying, "Get out of my house!"

I wondered what made him so angry with her. I loved living there and did not want to leave, I saw him as my father… he was a good man.

I knew for sure we would be moving! It was obvious she was upset over the altercation, but I knew she loved him, and we did not have anywhere else to go. Thank God, we continued to stay there, and they acted as if nothing ever happened while going on with day-to-day life as usual.

My stepdad was a kind and selfless man and would do anything for anybody, especially friends and family. He enjoyed drinking and having a good time. They loved playing loud oldies (but goodies), laughing, and partying. It was how they entertained company and we learned a lot of the 70's music after listening to it every night. There were a lot of ups, downs, good days and bad days, but they loved one another and he genuinely loved us.

I became used to living with my stepdad. It had been months and we were still there, which was quite unusual to be in the same place for a long period of time. I never could get too comfortable in one place for long because something always caused us to have to move. I would often think about everything that happened while we lived with our relatives, and I believed we were so much better off in comparison to those previous living situations. Spending family time and having dinner together every night brought some normalcy into my life.

Ready or Not

My mother's belly was so big, she was excited and ready to deliver. She and my stepdad had been planning for the arrival of their baby girl. They went clothes shopping to prepare for the baby's birth, buying all the cutest little outfits and bassinet, everything the baby would need to come home to. My mother must have sensed the baby would be coming soon because she had the baby bag packed and ready by the door. All we needed was the baby!

It was one of those chilly, yet sunny, clear skies kind of days in November, my mother started having pain and it appeared the time had finally arrived. She had to be taken to the hospital. When my stepdad came back home later that evening, he told us it was not quite time for the baby just yet, but my mother had to stay in the hospital for some type of complications with her high blood pressure. I was a little disappointed, but I worried about my mother, hoping she would be okay and soon have the baby.

With my mother being in the hospital and my stepdad working, he had one of his friends occasionally stay in the home to help watch us. We still had to attend school, even though I wished I could have been with my mother. I did as much as I could around the house and for my siblings. At this point, I was 9 years old and wanted my mother to hurry up and have the baby so she could come back home! After the sexual, physical, and emotional trauma I endured with my other relatives, I was afraid to be left with my stepdad's friend. Men scared me and made me feel uncomfortable. I did not want any reminders of *that relative*. The times he would be around I purposely stayed close to my brother so I would not be with him alone.

My stepdad's friend would tell me I was pretty, and all I could think was, *what's next?* I no longer wanted to hear I was "pretty;" it seemed to be followed by someone touching me and it made me feel awkward. I just wanted to be a kid, but how could I when adult things were happening to me all of the time? I was emotionally confused about what I had gone through and I tried to forget my reality. I felt different from everybody else because of it. Running away was not an option, although I wished it were.

<u>Up in Flames</u>

One Saturday afternoon while my stepdad was at work, we were home with his friend again. My brother decided to play with matches in a downstairs bedroom, which caused a small fire. My stepdad's friend was upstairs and I ran to tell him and in a panic he rushed to the fire and attempted to put it out with water.

It was unsuccessful. Fire and smoke spread quickly in that room and then through the back area of the house. We all made it out until I realized my sister never came downstairs behind us. She was only 5 years old. Once I saw she was not outside, before I knew it, I ran back into the house to get her from where she was hiding, upstairs in the front bedroom. We both became trapped and could not make it back downstairs because the smoke was too thick. I could hear yelling, "Monica run out of the house!"

I was holding my sister tightly and we were both crying and scared, too afraid to move as the smoke was coming closer and closer toward us.

All of a sudden, my stepdad's friend grabbed us. He came out of nowhere and ran us through the smoke downstairs and out the front door—he saved our lives! Once we made it outside, the fire trucks and so many people were around. We were coughing and choking but thankfully, we did not need to be hospitalized.

I remember seeing my stepdad run down the street, as he did not work too far from his home. I will never forget how happy he was to see us all out of the home in one piece; he was hugging and holding us, crying. I am sure he was hurt to see his home on fire, but us being alive and safe meant more.

We were temporarily without a place to stay and my stepdad had to think quickly. For one, he had to tell my mother, who was still in the hospital. I was told she was so upset after learning of the house fire. All she cared about was making sure her children were alive and okay. The thought of, *"What if my babies had died in that house fire"* was so overwhelming that I believed it caused her to go into labor, and my baby sister was born shortly thereafter.

After the fire, we stayed a couple days with my stepdad's mother while he handled business with the insurance company. He knew my mom wouldn't want to live there with his mother, so we needed a place to live when she and my sister were released from the hospital. My stepdad remained with his mother but quickly found us this small second-floor, two-bedroom apartment. It wasn't much but it was our own, finally.

A few days later my mother and baby sister were released from the hospital. I was so happy to see her; it seemed like she was gone forever! Plus, I was so excited seeing my sister for the first time— she was adorable! After a few weeks into our apartment and starting completely over, I felt good to be in our new place. A new neighborhood, school, and meeting friends were a normal part of our life; we were used to new beginnings. But this was the first place we had of our own.

ᴛʜᴇUNVEILING

It was not too long before my mother was back in the streets, maybe a month or so. She left me home to care for an infant, my brother who was one year younger than me, and my 5-year-old sister. I was used to her hanging out and partying but I was hoping the baby would keep her home a little while longer. I loved my mother so much but I didn't understand her decision making and thought process as a parent. I didn't question her when she would leave us alone because she always came back, I just never knew when.

I wanted to be a normal kid again, but somehow that part of my life got replaced with the responsibilities I wasn't ready for. Somehow, I became a mom and was forced to take on the role of an adult and I had no real clue about what I was doing. Having fun was something I rarely got a chance to do because I was pulled into adulthood and someone my age was too young to make decisions for their younger siblings. What was I supposed to do with an infant? I was only 9 years old myself, but I was changing diapers, making bottles, cooking, and cleaning.

One Friday evening while on school break, my mother had been gone for some days, and we were scared and hungry. We did not have a telephone, so I went to the corner phone booth to call my aunt because we needed food and the baby ran out of milk, I didn't know what else to do. I asked a man for some change and had him dial my aunt's number because I was too short to reach the phone on my own. After he dialed the number, he gave me the telephone and I told my aunt we were home alone and hungry. She was furious and came to take us back to her home because I should have never been left to run a household and take care of my siblings, especially not a baby.

Eventually, when my mom returned home to find us not there, she called her sister (my aunt) and was told that we were there at her house. She was not that fond of her picking us up, but at the same time I felt we were abandoned and needed help. But she never wanted my aunt "in her personal business," as she would say.

After a day or two, my aunt took us back home, but I didn't want to go back, I was unhappy there. I never knew why my mom stayed out in the streets, leaving me to care for my siblings. Acting like an adult was not what I wanted to do; however, I had no choice but to do things adults were doing. Somehow, I found myself in these uncompromising situations I couldn't control. I didn't believe I could be a child at all; I was more of a built-in babysitter and parent to my younger siblings, instead of a sister. I had already experienced things as a child I never should have, things I wanted to forget and bury.

<u>Thoughts of my Father</u>

Often, I wondered where my brother and I's father were. I knew it had to be hard on my mother raising her children by herself. Although my younger sister's father was around to help, it didn't stop me from wanting to know where my dad was. Maybe if he were around, she wouldn't leave me alone all of the time, well that's what I told myself. I guess this was just my way of thinking and believing he could've changed things.

My mother had shared stories with my brother and me about our dad periodically and she too hoped one day we would see him. He was around during the earlier part of our lives, but nothing we remembered, we were too young and it had been some years since he'd seen us. I do remember her telling me that when I was about 1 years old my dad attempted to take me to New York City without her permission. She called it kidnapping! However, that plan failed and he ended up bringing me back. The reality of dragging a 1-year-old around was probably too much for him to handle. I'm still not sure if it really was a kidnapping or if he just refused to bring me back after an argument—either way, it didn't change how desperate I was to meet my father. My brother was not as interested in seeing or knowing our father, at least it wasn't verbally expressed. I felt I needed him in my life. Little girls need their dad, and I wanted mine for various reasons.

I always wanted to know my father and I had a picture of him in my mind because my mom had a vivid description of him. She actually said he reminded her of Smokey Robinson and could sing like him too! The thoughts of being a daddy's little girl and bonding with him were something I one day hoped came true. I needed my father around in my life to slow things down because I was moving at a fast pace. There were so many things I wanted to say to him, but more importantly I wanted to know if he loved me. I just wished he knew how hard things had been for me. I missed feeling like a child. I wanted to know what it was like to have fun again like I used to with my cousins when Grandma Anna was alive. I was so disconnected from my childhood!

He Was Coming to Town

I will never forget the day when out of nowhere my father's cousin came to our house telling my mom he was on his way to Baltimore from Virginia. *Who, my father?* Can you imagine my excitement? I felt like a genie had jumped out of a bottle and my one wish had been granted. Thoughts ran through my mind: *What does he look like in real life? Will he be happy to see me? Will he stay forever?* I could not wait to see him, touch him, and hug him.

I couldn't believe it was finally going to happen. I was hoping it was true and he really was coming. I waited a long time for that moment, and I did not want to be disappointed. *Maybe I needed to calm down, but how could I—my father was coming!*

I waited at the window because we knew he was on the way. I had dreamt of that day and now at 9 years old I was meeting my father for the first time essentially. It was a cold winter night, but I felt the warmth of a Summer day running through my body. The anticipation of waiting for my daddy mixed with feelings of sadness because I wondered, *What if he doesn't show?* Finally, I saw a car pull up with several people inside and park right in front of our apartment. When this man stepped out of that car, I almost broke my neck running down the steps! I knew it was him—my mother's description of him was perfect. My mother was just as excited and my brother showed little emotion, but I jumped in his arms like he was the father of the year— to me, he was. He was just as happy to see my brother and I, smiling and telling us how much he loved and missed us. We were toddlers the last time he saw us. He spent every day with us during his short stay, taking us around his family as he visited with them. I didn't want to leave his presence. I was amazed at how much my brother and I resembled him; it was like looking into a mirror.

Seeing him for the first time was magical. Although I had never seen him, I loved him so much because I did not understand how not to love him, and when my mother talked about him, she never said anything negative.

I had dreamt of that exact moment. I needed him to rescue me from the hurt he didn't know existed, love me like his little girl, talk to me as his princess, and hold on to me like never before. I wanted him to say, "Daddy is here, and no one will ever hurt you again."

I loved my father so much; he was everything I imagined. I was overexcited and wanted to hold on to every memory. I knew one day I *would* see him. He always existed to me, and I waited for him.

His visit was only for a couple weeks before he had to return home to Virginia. I did not want him to leave because I knew it would be a long time before I saw him again, if at all. I held onto every waking moment I had with him, scared to let go, knowing that could be the last time. I wanted to tell him all that I was experiencing because he was my father and needed to know how I had been hurt. But I never shared my pain with him; I only enjoyed the time I had getting to know him, no matter how brief. His smile, laugh, and voice as he looked at me and called me his baby girl was priceless. I marveled at every word; I wanted nothing to interfere with those moments. I wanted to stop time because it was moving too fast getting closer to the time for him to leave.

My father had another name my family called him—"Champ." He was most definitely a real champ to me. I just wish he didn't have to return home. When it was time for him to go my heart was broken and I cried, begging him to stay. *Daddy please don't leave.* He assured me and my brother he would stay in touch with us. For that short bit of time, I felt safe like a shield of protection was around and nobody would be able to hurt me ever again. Unbeknownst to him, he left me feeling stranded and alone on a deserted island, frightened, and unprotected. *I regretted not telling him I had been sexually abused!*

CHAPTER 4

DROWNING DEEP

(Trying Not to Sink)

***We Carry These Things Inside Us. That No One Else Can
See. They Hold Us Down Like Anchors They Drown Us
Out At Sea.***
—Author Unknown

Weeks had gone by and I was missing my father terribly, we talked here and there, but it was not enough. I wanted more time with him, I wanted forever with my father. I had not seen him in my life as he had seen me in my earlier years and I was not ready to let go of him again. I was hoping he'd come back soon, so I was left holding on to what I had: his hug, his smile, and his time.

But we had more important matters to tend to. My mother could no longer afford the apartment and we were about to get evicted. Once again, we needed another place to live—please no more family members, I did not trust them. Where would we go, a family of five possibly being cramped into one bedroom or sleeping on someone's floor?

My mother shared with a male friend, Mr. B., that we were about to be evicted and coincidentally he knew a friend who was renting out a third-floor bedroom. My mother got in touch with the lady, Ms. M., and she offered her the room; however, she only would allow my mother and two children.

How do you put a mother in a situation to choose which two of her four children to bring along? What happens with the other two? My mother had to act fast and make a decision before Ms. M. changed her mind. Mr. B. came up with a brilliant plan to take my brother and me until her living situation changed. She hesitated but agreed, feeling there was no choice in the matter. I wondered why my mother did not let my brother and me temporarily stay with her sister; maybe she had her reasons, other than her saying my aunt was nosey.

Mr. B. was a good man and he treated us nicely. He had a glass eye. I saw him take out one time and it freaked me out; other than that, I thought he was perfect. He took us to drive-in movies, bowling, and out for food on occasions. We had fun with him! When we were separated from our mother to live with Mr. B, we had no idea how to feel about not living with her; no matter what we never lived separately regardless of how many times we moved around. Being with my mother was all we knew we had never been apart. But with no other option, my brother and I went off to a fresh start to live with our new family.

Mr. B. lived with a Caucasian family of five—a husband and wife and their three children (two girls and a boy)—in a nice, big house. We all got along, and after a while my brother and I adjusted, and we loved it. We never wanted to go back to live with our mother. I especially did not want to because finally I was able to enjoy my childhood again. We were allowed to visit her on the weekends, but we could not wait to go back home on Sunday evening. I looked around and it felt good to be having fun like a kid with nothing to worry about! It was nice being 10 years old and not being responsible for taking care of my siblings or being touched or someone hurting me sexually. Mr. B. loved us and treated us like we were his own children. Deep down inside I saw him as a father because he fulfilled the role a daddy should've. He brought our first bikes and new clothes for school, and all I wanted was to feel safe with someone I trusted. I was already feeling like something in me had changed and wanted to turn off all the negative thoughts in my head.

The family we lived with enjoyed having us around; we ate meals together, laughed, played outside like kids do, and watched movies as a family. I was living a dream life being a kid without any responsibilities… something I was not used to.

Every night we took our baths, put our pajamas on, and I would sleep in the girl's room and my brother with the boy. After a couple of months, Mr. B. suddenly changed my sleeping arrangements. I could no longer sleep with the girls, but my brother continued to sleep in the same place. Mr. B. slept in one part of the basement while the son and my brother slept in a separate area of the basement.

One night, after my bath, Mr. B. told me it was okay not to sleep in my pajamas and to sleep in his bed. I said ``Okay,'' without any thought.

There was no reason to question him or think something was wrong, as a child I did what I was told. It was the middle of the night and I remember being awakened to Mr. B. pulling my panties down and sticking the tip of his penis in my private area, not all the way but just enough. I did not want to believe it was happening again; I trusted Mr. B. As I laid there silently crying, he whispered, "Shhhhhh."

I could hear him softly moaning as the tears rolled down my face, I wondered why Mr. B would hurt me too? Taking it out of me is what I wanted him to do. It was painful! Afterwards, I tried to fall asleep as I cried to myself, thinking something was wrong with me. The next morning I went on with the day as if I was alright, but I was hurting. I wanted my days to last longer because my nights were too painful.

For weeks he continued to molest me. I felt so disgusting and no bath could clean me, nothing could take away the smell of his breath on my neck or the pain of his penis partially inside me. I screamed and cried for my brother's help one night, but my voice was silent and nothing came out. I wanted it to stop and more importantly I wanted my mother, my father, anybody to come get me. Another secret I was forced to keep, I was not sure if I could. But I did not want him to get in trouble.

In the morning, he would look me in the face as if nothing ever happened and I would look at him right back with fear and shame. *What did I do again to deserve this?* My young body had endured so much; I did not want another man to call me pretty because it was associated with pain and violation. I wanted to be ugly, then maybe no man would want me. What struck me the most was how Mr. B acted as if he had done nothing wrong.

One weekend, while visiting our mother, I told the granddaughters of Ms. M. about what Mr. B. was doing to me. I don't know why I broke my silence to them and didn't keep the secret as I was told to do. We were close in age and had become friends when I would visit my mom on the weekends. I confided in them and they told their mother, who then told my mother. When my mother asked me about it, I was so scared to admit it, but I did. The look of rage on her face and the curse words that came out of her mouth were frightening. She stormed out of that house saying, "I am going to kill that motherfucker."

She and Mrs. Q. (Ms. M.'s daughter) went to his job, which was not that far from where my mother lived and tried to do exactly what she said (kill him). When she returned back to the house, my mother was still furious and she wanted answers. I was so ashamed and afraid to talk about the abuse to her. She wanted to know how long, when did it start, why didn't I tell her... my only answer was, "He told me it was a secret."

If only I could have mustered enough strength to tell her about the other secret I was keeping. I wanted it all to go away, discussing it made me feel worse.

My mother met with the family we were living with to tell them about what Mr. B. had done to me and they were devastated. They were so surprised by what was happening under their roof. They kept telling my mother and me how sorry they were as the tears rolled down their faces and mine. They wished I had told them. Mr. B was not home at the time, but the father was so angry and could not control the rage he was feeling, he wanted to hurt him and yelled that he wanted to press charges. Now they were left wondering what type of man had been invited into their home and family. Mr. B. was not welcomed to live with them and we were assured he had to move out of their home immediately. They actually wanted my brother and me to stay but my mother no longer wanted us to. Us staying with them was not her choice to begin with; she had been in a desperate situation. We packed our clothes and off we went to move with our mom and I had never been so happy.

I never saw Mr. B. or that family again. It was a relief not seeing him; he had become a monster, but I was heartbroken over not being able to see that family who took us in too. Looking back now, I wish I had not been afraid to tell my mother about that relative who had sexually abused me too, especially after knowing how she handled Mr. B., but I kept quiet because he was family. At least I was protected from Mr. B. ever hurting me again. After the commotion in the store and learning what he had done, we later found out Mr. B was fired from his job. I'm not sure if my mom pressed any charges against him, but I do not believe she did because I was never questioned by a police officer. I was too young to have that conversation about whether or not he should be arrested and charged, that was left up to my mother.

I was glad to know Ms. M. immediately told my mom we could come there once finding out what I'd been through. My life had been redefined as a child and I questioned my position. I was no longer feeling like the little innocent girl that had been taken away from me. I knew I had to now trust new people, friends, school, and myself. I was not enjoying my childhood. I was missing parts of what that should look like.

Although, I was glad to be back with my mother, my brother and I really missed that family and seeing them. We spoke to them a few times after we moved away until the communication faded away altogether.

Ms. M. was strict, and she did not play any games. Her rules were set in stone and breaking them was not an option. Her boyfriend and wheelchair-bound brother, Mr. E., lived in the home too. I feared men, believing they all wanted something from me—sex. Sadly, after everything, I just wanted to hide and not be seen, I felt shameful. I was so scared of getting in trouble, thinking I did not do something right and that's why those things happened to me. I thought it was my fault, I could have done something to stop Mr. B and *that* relative, like scream or fight, but I did nothing.

Mr. E. would look at me and wink his eyes. This was the beginning of something familiar. *Not again.* He was a creepy man with missing teeth and in a wheelchair. When he saw me alone or coming out of the bathroom, he would wheel himself close to me and say, "Come here little girl," and I would go to him.

He would grab me, and I could not pull away once he had a tight grip on me. He was disabled, but strong. He would squeeze me close to him and rub my body on his body, saying, "Make me feel good."

What did that mean, I thought to myself?

Why did my mother have to always be away from us leaving me vulnerable and unprotected? Was this my fault too that Mr. E. would take out his penis, grab my hand, and make me rub it as he made sounds? He was in a wheelchair I should have pulled away, but he had control. Did it mean I liked it? It was harder to understand than a 10 year old should have had to figure out. I always felt in danger; I never felt safe and comfortable no matter where I was.

I did not want us getting put out; I did not know what else to do. We did not have anywhere else to live and I was too scared that had I said something, Ms. M would have told us we had to leave. I had a nervous feeling around Mr. E. afterward. I was not safe around him or anyone else, for that matter. I could not explain these acts of violation that seemed to happen to me everywhere I went.

I knew my mother was happy to have my brother and me back with her; but I wanted to run away and never come back. I was always responsible for too much, being left alone without proper parental supervision, which is why I was such an easy target for abuse. Although Ms. M and her boyfriend were home, they stayed mostly on the first level and Mr. E. spent the majority of his time on the second floor. Our living space was on the third floor, and we did not go downstairs when our mother was not home, only to eat or use the bathroom. I hated going to the bathroom because Mr. E. was always in the hallway in his wheelchair. I did my best to stay away from him; I tried not to use the bathroom often or would ask my brother to go with me and wait outside the door. He would do it, but not without asking why. I would tell him I was scared of the hallway.

My mother often left us with Ms. M., and I would watch my siblings, which I was used to doing. We stayed with Ms. M for about two years before moving into our own home again. I could not wait to move away from that house! At times, it was unbearable, I was so tired of living with people who I could not trust. As we prepared for our new house, my mother called that relative who molested me to help us move—yup, he was right there, always willing to help. She had no idea of the harm he had inflicted on me and something was telling me it was not over.

How would I ever be able to feel normal with him coming around?

He did not have any boundaries—none of the perpetrators did. My mother trusted him; she had no reason not to. She was not going to forbid him from being near me since she was unaware of what he had done. At that point, I stopped knowing what was right or wrong, I was just ready to move and hoped I would be able to put it all behind me. It was hard to process my feelings and put into words what I had been through! For me, it was a never-ending nightmare that I wanted to wake up from. I was a kid growing up around people I had encountered so much hurt and disappointment from. There was a lot more I didn't know about life and I wasn't sure if I wanted to.

CHAPTER 5
COMPLEX SITUATIONS

(Everything in Question)

Life is too complex to compress into soundbites. Every situation is different.
—Sarah Brightman

We moved into a nice, three-bedroom house in East Baltimore in a quiet neighborhood. The neighbors at the corner house became like family to us. A mother and father lived there with their five children (four daughters and one son), who were young adults and their youngest daughter was a teenager. Although we became close with other people on the block, we always felt more involved with them. We spent quite a bit of time sitting outside on their front steps, especially during the Summer. They would keep a close eye on the house during the times they knew my mother would leave us home alone.

My mother was very cordial, so it did not take long before she had become friends with people on the same street. I loved living there and getting to know more new faces, but I was always wondering how long we would stay. I was not the same after what I had been put through, it was starting to bother me more and it was not fading away. My life was unfolding before me and it was not looking bright and blooming for me.

While living there, I had formed a strong attraction to my neighbor's son; he was about 19 years old and good-looking. I wanted him to notice me, but he only saw me as a little girl. He knew I liked him because I made childlike, indirect advances at him and being bashfully flirtatious. He would smile and say, "You are too young, give it a few more years, like when you're 18."

I could not understand why he did not want me; all the others did. Was I not pretty enough for him? Everywhere I lived some man had put his hands or body parts on me in places they never should have. I guess I wanted him to look at me as someone his age, but instead I went unnoticed. Why was I having these unprecedented feelings or interest in sex anyway?

Return of the Bogeymen

With all the compromising situations I had been in, I was taught things about sex I otherwise would not have known. My innocence had been violated and that took me on a path in the wrong direction. I was 13 years old, and found myself with strong desires for men. Due to my traumatizing experiences, I had lost my ability to conduct myself as a child.

Any male friend or boyfriend my mother brought to the house made me want to run away and hide; I would shiver on the inside with fear. But then, on the other hand, I wanted to be seen. Being around men made me feel like that 7-year-old little girl and I was anxious all the time. I had developed a nervousness from the abuse, which caused me to be on high alert watching and waiting for the next thing to happen. I wanted to act like the child I knew I was, but acting much older than my age seemed right, it was unexplainable. Vulnerable and frightened was an internal and external struggle that should have easily been seen by my mother. Sometimes in the same room with her I did not feel safe around family and especially men. I saw how they would look at me and it made me worried and uneasy because I thought something inappropriate or bad would end up happening. I was up and down with my emotions; one minute I was a scared little girl and the next it seemed like I wanted the attention.

My mom had this one male friend, Mr. M., who was a truck driver and always on the road but made time to stop by when he was in the area. Mr. M. was friendly, pleasant, and loved bringing my mother takeout food. He was tall, dark, and handsome, as she would describe him, "A good looking man."

One day, he was over at the house and my mother went to take a bath to get ready to go out with him. She invited him to come upstairs to wait in her bedroom where I was sitting on the bed watching television. Now why would she do that? Immediately, I became anxious as he started off with small talk, but there was something about the way he was staring at me. He said, "Come here and sit on my lap," and so I did. I was doing as I was told as I usually did. He said, "You are a pretty young thing, you know that?"

Nervously smiling and shaking at the same time, I answered yes, not knowing what he would do next—or maybe I did...

Mr. M. pulled me close and kissed me on the lips while running his fingers through my hair. At that moment I knew he would hurt me like the others. *How long would it be before my mother finished with her bath?* I wanted her to hurry before Mr. M went any further with me.

Whatever it was that men liked about me, I wanted it to go away. We heard my mother getting out of the tub and Mr. M. gently stood me up from his lap. As soon as she walked in to get dressed, I went downstairs saying nothing about the kiss.

During one of his visits prior to the kiss, I asked if my brother and I could go for a ride in his 16-wheeler truck and of course he said, "Yes, as long as your mother is okay with it."

He would come around in that big truck with those huge wheels honking his horn; I thought it would be fun to go for a ride. I'd never seen a truck that big before and to a child that was fascinating.

My mother said it was okay so my brother and I could not wait— until the time came to go and my brother was not home. All I could think about was that kiss. Mr. M. said, "Are y'all ready for the ride?"

My brother was not there, and I did not want to go alone. He said, "You can still come along."

"I do not want to go now," I said to my mother.
Please do not force me to go, I said to myself. She told him maybe another time and I was happy. I can only imagine how disappointed he was that I did not ride in his truck alone without my brother.

I didn't see too much of him anymore after that, but I know my mother met him out a couple of times. I was not mad he wasn't coming around anymore—one less person for me to worry about.

I was feeling trapped in that cycle of abuse and being forced to do things I did not want to do. I was tired of being someone whom others felt the need to touch. I didn't even know how to ask for help, always finding a way to protect the perpetrators, I was incapable of defending myself against those who harmed me. I started to normalize and accept the abuse. I often felt invisible like I was being overlooked by the one person who was supposed to see me, my mother. I did not want any of this, but I often felt I deserved it. Maybe I was acting too grown and drawing attention to myself. I had been so disappointed from my childhood and not understanding why it went wrong or knowing how to live as a child should. The constant worries, lack of trust, and questions were looming, which made it even more difficult to articulate my thoughts. I had gone through things no child should have ever experienced.

That relative would find his way around to our house regularly dropping in. "I was in the neighborhood," he would say.

My mother never noticed the fear in my eyes when he was present. I wanted to tell her what he had done and was still doing to me… I just did not know how. Maybe if I told her, she would stop allowing him to come over. It was difficult having to be around him because I knew what he'd do when her back was turned or if she left the room. The quick feels and kisses, and if she took long enough, fondled my private area. At that point, he knew I was not going to say anything, which made it easier for him to keep doing it, he became emboldened. He did not seem bothered by what he was doing or had done to me, he continued acting like his ordinary self. My mother had no idea of the type of person he really was. It was the hardest thing for me because I felt like the problem and he was labeled as the good old Christian man everyone looked up to. It was awkward, but I had to bury it and try to forget about it. This went on for many more years.

<u>Nowhere Was Safe</u>

There was a strange darkness in my family. I still had scars and open wounds from the other's that inflicted pain onto me. And yet, things continued happening to me that I could not make sense of or express in words.

One afternoon, I was walking home from school and another relative who lived fairly close to our house saw me while he was standing in his doorway. He asked me to come over, so I did. I was familiar with him but did not know him well, but I had been in his company before during family gatherings. I had no idea why he asked me to come in, but I gave it little to no thought as I should have. While inside, he was asking how my mother was doing, showing me old pictures of family, and making small talk—seemed harmless.

Next, he led me into the dining area. Nothing appeared too strange until he started touching me inappropriately, and again I found myself doing what I was told to do.

The Unwanted Touching

I did not put up much of a fight as he laid me on the floor and got on top of me, pulled my shirt up, took out his penis and, as I know now, masturbated until he released himself all over my chest. I just laid there stiff; I did not know what was going on. I was scared and confused and then it was over. Afterward, he just wiped my chest off as if what he did was not unusual and told me not to tell anyone. So I didn't.

After the other incidents, should I have known better? He was not a stranger and neither were the others! Was I drawing the wrong kind of attention? If so, then how? Was it the way I walked, looked, smiled or laughed... What was it? When I complied, did I give permission? I did not say "stop" or "no"... did that mean yes? I never knew how to feel or think; my to-do list did not involve fighting off men and stopping them from sexually violating me. It was never my responsibility to put grown men in their place or to tell them what they were doing was wrong. I was tired of being around men that touched me in places they should not have had access to. None of this made any sense to me at all, I was kid, with no real childhood and around a bunch of inexplicable people.

After that incident, I left and went home like nothing happened; I was used to keeping secrets and protecting those who hurt me. I was embarrassed and humiliated. I knew I had to explain to my mom why I was late coming home from school. I rehearsed what I was going to say during my walk home—a lie. I was afraid of not being heard, so I silenced my voice, keeping what needed to be said buried inside. I did not want to cause any problems in the family. Who would believe a bizarre story like that anyway?

The way he lured me in his house was very strategic: "Hey, how are you? How is your mom?"

He seemed innocently concerned, asking about my school day. "Come in, I want to show you something." How could he do this to me like it was no big deal, how could this keep happening? It was just too much and I did not like my family member's.

No one in my family seemed trustworthy and I did not want them in my life. I really became fearful, not knowing if I should tell and wondering who would believe me. My abuse started when I was seven years old by someone I knew and trusted, and what this relative did was no different. In the wake of all the abuse, I was left to bear the burden and hurt alone. I was so confused about my role as a child, I had no idea what I was supposed to do as a little girl anymore. I had no other choice but to keep quiet, and I did! Sadly, I felt there was no one to talk to about my feelings.

By the time I celebrated my 13th birthday, I felt out of place like I was mentally too mature for people my age. I had the body of a little girl but the mind of a mature adult. I so desperately wanted to be a child, but the people around me would not let me. I did not ask for any of this to happen to me. I continued to find myself in the worst situations, never feeling safe enough, not even in my own skin.

Trouble All Around Me

Then there was Mr. C., an old man my mother would borrow money from. He lived a few doors up from our house. Not sure why she would send me to ask him every time but being the oldest child, I was expected to do things all of the time. Mr. C. was a widower in his late 70s, maybe 80s. My mom would say, "Go ask Mr. C. if I could borrow [whatever amount she needed at the time] dollars,".

It's not like I could refuse what she asked me to do, although I did not want to go. As a child, you listen to your parents, not asking any questions, doing as you were told. She always paid him back as promised, but after a few times it seems he saw me as payment.

I'd gone to his house again to ask for another loan for my mother and he asked me to come in while he got the money; usually, I waited outside the door. As he put the money in my hand, he rubbed my chest. He was a nasty old man, and I did not want to go there again, but I had to when my mother borrowed money from him.

The fears I developed as a little girl were overwhelmingly stressful and had taken a toll on me causing strong feelings of distrust. I hated knocking on his door because I knew something I could not control was going to happen and it did. He laid on the sofa pulling me on top of him, kissing my lips, moving my body on top of his. I could smell the snuff tobacco on his breath as he told me I was making him feel good. I wanted to cry. I felt powerless and the world did not feel safe. *Did I deserve being mistreated like this? Was this normal?*

I had to tell my mother, so she'd stop sending me and finally I said, "Ma, Mr. C. touched my breasts, kissed me, and put me on top of him." Surely, she would not send me again, right? Wrong. "You're all right. He's old, he cannot hurt you," she said.

But he was. It did not make sense to me why she thought that was okay because he was old. That made telling her about those relatives, the kiss from Mr. M and what Mr. E did more difficult. I thought she would storm up there and knock Mr. C out no matter how old he was. I felt abandoned and disappointed.

I wanted to run away from everything and everyone but there was no escaping. The wrong that seemed right to other people was growing increasingly confusing in the eyes of a 13-year-old girl, and I was becoming angry. The world and everyone in it seemed crazy. I saw those men around me as people I should have been able to trust; instead, they took advantage of me. They somehow made me believe that they cared about me. Not knowing that I was being manipulated and groomed. In those times, it was nearly impossible for me to see how I had been trained to trust the people who were planning to hurt me beyond repair. I just wanted it to end, feeling so weak and vulnerable not knowing how I could stop the abuse?

The Icing on the Cake

At this time, I was a young teenager. This was an important age for me and I wanted to enjoy these teenage years. I felt differently from my peers. It was a pain deep inside that was difficult to explain. I had been robbed of my innocence and was feeling helpless. I wanted to deny myself of the truth, but something real had been taken from me that I would never get back, my childhood.

After all I was going through, I later found out my mom was on drugs. I was a young girl. What was I supposed to do after learning about that newfound information? Drugs were not a topic of conversation I'd ever had with my mother or anybody else. I was unaware of what all that meant, therefore my reaction to it was that of ignorance. I mean, really was I supposed to confront her about it?

As if telling me my mother was on drugs was not enough my neighbor also told me that my mom was selling her food stamps in exchange for money to buy the drugs. It made sense as she tried to explain it to me on my level of understanding, yet still confusing. I did notice there were certain times of the month we did not have as much groceries in the refrigerator. But I thought nothing of it, definitely not that. I was not keeping track or paying attention as to why we did not have food. I just knew there were times when we did not and was left trying to figure it out. Things were happening around me, which left many questions that I did not have the answers to.

We grew up on public assistance; that was all I ever knew. My mom did not work a 9-to-5, but she took pride in taking care of us as best she could. I was unaware at the time of what she did or did not do with her money. I know she made sure we had mostly what we needed for school, Easter, and what little Christmas shopping she could do for my siblings and I. My mother was very frugal. She only bought what was necessary and we always appreciated what little we had. We knew not to question her by asking for more.

My mother was a private woman, she would say, "What happens in this house stays in this house."

She never wanted us to talk about her business, as she would call it. I learned how to lie when those bill collectors would call—"Tell them I'm not here"—or when my mother's sister would call. She called her nosey and said my aunt only wanted to "be in her business." So I most definitely was not about to tell my aunt that my mother had started using drugs. Unfortunately, my younger childhood years were taken and now my teenage years were already in complete disarray and I had no idea what to do about it.

Who else's life was as hard as mine, I wondered? Roadblocks were no surprise to me, always something getting in the way. With everything else, now my mom was on drugs! I did not have a conversation with her about what I was told and surely she was not going to discuss it with me. I did not know what signs to look for. How does someone on drugs look? I did not know what to think about all of this and who was going to help me understand, and was this going to change our life even more? Was this the beginning to an end? Was my mother going to die from drugs? I was scared and this inflamed my fears.

Growing Up Too Fast

I went through a period of finding myself wanting to be needed, and so I attached myself to anyone who showed a love interest in me. Essentially, I became blinded by my own desperate need to get attention. I could not feel the rope around my neck pulling me in the direction of young men, but it was definitely there. They wanted me all of the time and I assumed it was because of my looks. When men violated me as a little girl, they would tell me how pretty I was, so I believed that would be the reason boys liked me.

I had my first boyfriend when I was 14 years old and he was nearly 20. I thought he would be the love of my life. I was 14; what did I really know about love? I can recall falling deeply in love after we first had sex. Thinking about him day and night waiting for the phone to ring, and hoping to see him every day. My mother had me on birth control because she said I was too "fast" and she did not want me getting pregnant. Although I was on birth control, I never admitted to my mom I was sexually active with him. She would ask me if I was having sex and I would say no. She noticed how much I liked him so she always assumed things had gone further.

I thought my boyfriend loved me as much as I loved him, but he was only using me. I eventually found out he had another girlfriend, which broke my heart. I am sure my mother knew I was not telling the truth about not having sex, especially by the way I responded to finding out he had been dishonest. I did not know what to do with those emotions after I stopped seeing him, so I buried them deep inside with everything else. What did I know about being loved by a man anyway? Those were the times when a girl needed her father the most.

A Much-Needed Break

After my heartbreak, I began to miss my father again. I wished he were there for me, maybe he could have been my shoulder to cry on. Although he was the first man to ever hurt me emotionally, I still needed him. I attempted to fill so many voids and one was his absence.

The last I saw him was about four to five years prior, when I first met him at 9 years of age. I asked my mother if there was any way of finding him again, but she was not sure. She must have pondered on my question and reached out to my father's side of the family concerning his whereabouts because after a few failed attempts, we got the break we needed—a telephone number to reach him. My brother did not care as much as I did about our father, so he showed little to no interest in talking to him. I was filled with joy as my mother and I walked to the corner phone booth to call my father.

Ring, ring, ring

"Hi daddy, this is your daughter," I said.

He was just as excited to hear my voice, as I was to hear his. I barely knew what to say to him but he had a lot of questions for me. Before we hung up, he asked if I wanted to spend the Summer with him, which was three months from then. I could not believe I was going to possibly spend the summer with my daddy! He told me he was married, and I had three younger sisters that he wanted me to meet. The 15-20 minute conversation felt like hours. It was wonderful, and then he asked to speak with my mother.

Before hanging up she gave me the phone so we could say goodbye. He told me I could call him as much as I wanted to. It was not long after then that my mother got another home phone installed and I was able to talk to him more. Every time we'd speak, something in my heart felt right; I just wanted my daddy.

He continued to assure me he was coming to get me for the summer. It was a big deal for me. I was hoping my mother did not change her mind about letting me go. I did not want to get my hopes up just in case he did not show up, but I couldn't help but to be anxious. I needed a break from the life I had been forced to live and I hoped my father could release me from it all just for a little while.

It was getting closer to the time he said he would come from

Virginia to get me and I was anticipating his arrival. I cared so much about my father although he was a stranger to me. I was focused on spending time with him and meeting my sisters.

School was out and summer had just begun, and it was one week before he was to come. I had never packed so many clothes before in my life. The day before he was coming, we talked and he said, "Baby Girl, are you ready?"

He called me "Baby Girl"!

"Yes," I said with excitement. "I cannot wait!"

He came to Baltimore and spent a few days with family, as well as my brother and I, before we traveled back to Virginia. I did not want to leave his side, fearing he would leave without me... but he didn't. I was so happy to see him again and I was glad to have been in communication with him prior to coming to help ease my doubts.

The day came for us to leave, I hugged my mother so tight as if I was never going to see her again. I had never been apart from her, other than the time when my brother and I lived with that other family; now I was going to a different state.

After arriving at my father's house and meeting his wife who had heard all about me, I was nervous about how she would treat me. His wife had two young adult children, a son and daughter, whom I spent a lot of time with as they showed me around the town. Our days on the beach, at concerts and movies, shopping and eating at restaurants were the best days of my life. It made me forget about everything unpleasant I had gone through. My father and his wife adored me, making me feel at home while attempting to make up for his years of not being in my life.

My mother called me frequently to make sure I was okay, but she also wanted to know how much longer I would stay. I was really missing her after a few weeks of being there, but I was not ready to go back just yet. It was like a dream for me to be with my father— one I did not want to ever forget. It felt good to live in the moment, something I had not been able to do in a long time.

Being with my father made me wonder if I would have gone through those experiences of sexual trauma had he been around. But I had to remain in a good place. What those men did to me was not my father's fault. I never held a grudge against him for not being there. I was enjoying my time and another great part of my trip was meeting two of my three younger sisters. Although my visit with them was brief due to the estranged relationship my dad had with their mother, meeting them could not have been any less precious and memorable.

After about five weeks, I was getting homesick. I did not want to leave my dad, but I wanted to go back home with my mother. I was also missing my siblings. I stayed another week and my father drove me back home, but I had the most amazing time; he made sure of it. After five-to-six hours on the road, I was back home.

My dad stayed in Baltimore for a few more days before going back home, and as soon as he left, I became extremely sad, almost feeling empty inside. Being with him meant everything to me, but the fact that I might not see him again made his absence more heartbreaking. However, summer was just about over, and high school was approaching. I was not sure if I was ready for this change; but I was excited to finally be entering high school! Thoughts of my father were always on my mind.

Transitioning

Boys were everywhere, and I could barely contain myself around them. Some of them looked older than high school kids—I was seeing muscles and mustaches everywhere. I did not want to get involved with anyone at the school, but I knew it would be a matter of time before I would. I just felt so weak, vulnerable, and inferior around boys, feeling like I had no sexual control. I wanted to be focused on schoolwork and not boys, but that attempt did not last long. After a couple of weeks, I had become so distracted with the boys at school, especially the ones who were showing interest in me. When I was with my father, it was unspoken, but I felt like I was forbidden to like boys, but that time was over.

I was attending one of the most popular high school's in town and some of the senior boys had their eyes on me, making it known that they wanted me. I got involved with a senior who was well liked and had been around with quite a few girls at the school. I was not sure how to be in a relationship, but I knew it involved sex. My idea of sex, men, and relationships had been influenced by the abuse as a child and it was tainted. When a guy asked for "it", you gave "it" up, even if you were not ready to.

When he initially approached me asking for my number, I felt special because I had something he wanted. I would go over to his house after school and would tell lies to my mother about where I was. I had become a master at not being honest from all the secrets I had been forced to keep. I was always making up lies because I did not want her knowing I was having sex, but she knew. I wanted to be somebody's favorite and only girl and thought sex would do that. He and I's relationship ended quickly; my emotional scarring caused me to have a difficult time trusting and committing.

I was filling my emptiness, pain, and hurt with sex as a result of the sexual abuse that I was pretending did not exist and was not happening. I tried to emotionally disconnect but the triggers were there to remind me. I became so rebellious doing stuff I was not supposed to be doing. I was angry at the world and full of rage with feelings of guilt, shame, and blame that I could not easily explain with words. My destructive behaviors only dominated my emotions further sending me deeper into a messy life.

Often, I reflected on my life and thought about if I could have done anything different to change what happened to me as a little girl. My life was not exactly what I hoped it to be, and I wondered if it would ever get better for me, but I was losing all hope of that happening. I was a complete wreck! My life was in shambles. I just wanted to be successful in high school and focus on those types of challenges. Moving on and forgetting was hard to do because *that* relative was still around and so was the abuse at times.

A Change Is Coming

One night when my mother and I were out she went into this bar while I waited for her outside. I was wearing a long white fitted skirt, a black blouse, and black shoes. My hair was in a layered tilt style and I was looking cute. This handsome man turned the corner and we stared at each other, quickly telling one another all types of nasty things with our eyes. I believed I was in the right place at the right time, and I wanted this man. He walked up to me asking my name. I answered, "Monica" while smiling from ear to ear.
He asked, "How old are you?"

I said, "17."

Not too far from the truth. I had just turned 15 but he did not need to know that. I was glad he did not ask for proof.
"How old are you?" I asked.

"20," he replied.

I wondered if he believed I was really 17; I did not care how old he was, I had to have this good-looking man. We exchanged numbers and I hoped he'd call fast.

My mom finally came out of the bar while we were still talking, and she waited. While we were walking back home, of course she asked whom I was talking to. Innocently smiling, I told her, "A guy I just met."

We talked briefly about it before moving on to something else. He was on my mind the entire walk home; his eyes were so beautiful with his caramel skin. I hoped he did not throw away my number; I honestly did not want to make the first move by calling him. I could not believe I was home an hour before my phone rang. Rushing to the phone, I answered, "Hello?"

It was him. My heart dropped.

ᵀᴴᴱUNVEILING

CHAPTER 6
TRYING TO ESCAPE

(Hiding in My Pain)

You're trying to escape from your difficulties, and there never is any escape from difficulties, never. They have to be faced and fought.
—Enid Blyton

I was looking for love in all the wrong places, trying to find it anywhere, everywhere, and from anybody. No one had truly understood what I had been through but me. I failed at every attempt to escape my past. I wanted to be free from all the pain, most of which others caused. I struggled within to emotionally heal; it was not as easy as I thought.

Answering the phone that night proved my point. It changed the trajectory of my life in an unimaginable way. We talked, but that was not enough. He wanted to see me and vice versa; in hindsight I do not think he was that interested in actually getting to know me. I remember sitting outside on my front steps on a nice spring night. He told me he was on his way, and I patiently waited.

I watched him walk down the street toward my house. This man was touching me with his eyes as he stared at me and dazzled me with his words right after. I could tell he wanted me! It didn't happen that night, but at our next encounter it did. The next time he came over, I snuck him in the house upstairs and into the bathroom. My heart was beating faster than a roadrunner bolting through the desert. He kissed me and laid me on the floor, pulling down my pants, and had sex with me with no protection like he loved me. Love was sex in my mind. Intimacy with him made me feel like a woman for some reason. I gave him the only thing every man was after—my body.

As we had sex, he was hurting me, but I did not make him stop. I just endured the pain; I became a master at masking my pain. Once it was over, he felt good but I was not too sure if I was supposed to experience the same thing or not. He told me that he came inside of me, but I did not know what that meant, but acted as if I did.

Life was moving fast; everything was spinning in circles and my hormones were out of control. I was a young girl growing into a woman and I did not know how to manage it all. I was screaming inside, yelling for help with a silent voice that no one could hear. The little girl inside was fighting to stay alive, starving for the love and attention she never got. She was a prisoner inside of my body. I wanted her to stay locked away, but deep inside she wanted a chance to be the child she never could be. I wanted him to see me as a woman and not that timid and fearful little girl whom men took advantage of. I did not want him to know the damaged girl, instead I wanted him to see that I was grown and mature.

I continued to see him and the next time we hooked up was at his house where he lived with his mother. He had a room in the basement. I knew he did not want to talk the entire night, so we didn't. Sex with him was different this time, it was on a bed and we did not feel rushed to finish. He held me afterward—something I was not used to. *Is that what people do?* I did not know. I went along with whatever he did—I knew how to follow rules—and then we both fell asleep briefly. I started to really like him; I thought I was falling in love again. But I knew nothing about how love was supposed to feel, only that it was a four-letter word with a meaning that made no sense to me.

The dictionary describes love as "An intense feeling of deep connection, a great interest and pleasure in something, feeling a deep romantic or sexual attachment to (someone)."

I believed I was experiencing that type of love, but was it real? The last time I thought I loved someone my heart was broken, and I could not be sure this man loved me, he never said he did. We had nothing more than sexual encounters, but was that not enough for love? I was not as experienced in sex and love as I thought I was. There was no real example to follow so I had no idea what to look for. Maybe his mind was different from mine. I did not know what conversation to have with him about love, so I followed his lead in the ... I didn't even know what to call us!

As time passed, something was happening to my body. I was extremely tired, falling asleep during the strangest of hours, eating more than usual, experiencing unexplained feelings of nausea. *Please do not let me be pregnant, my mother would kill me.* I heard the words loudly in my head, "You better not get pregnant because you cannot live here! I am not raising a child!"

I believed my mother's words and I was afraid. Even though she put me on birth control, I was not taking them as I was instructed to. I did not feel comfortable telling her the truth about sex, so I continued to deny it. My mother recognized how exhausted I had suddenly become and realized I was not using sanitary napkins during what should have been my monthly menstrual time.

"Monica, have you had your period?"

"Yes."

"What sanitary napkins are you using?

"I had some left over."

"Really," she said. "I am taking you to the doctor and you better not be pregnant."

I had to confess I had been sexually active because what if I were pregnant? She cussed and yelled at me once again saying, "You better not be pregnant because I am not taking care of any babies!"

So many thoughts ran through my mind: *What am I going to do with a baby (even though I had taken care of my siblings since I was 7 years old)? I guess I would take care of my own baby the same way. I do not have a job; I'm in high school. Where will I live? Who will help me? Wait—I have to tell the father of this child!*

Off to the doctor's appointment we went. I was examined and had to take a pregnancy test. While I anxiously waited, I was shaking and afraid to hear the outcome. Then the doctor said, "You are 16 weeks pregnant."

I knew it, but I did not want to believe it. *What does 16 weeks pregnant mean exactly?*

"You are four months along in your pregnancy."

The doctor asked to speak with my mother since I was a minor. I knew my mom would not take the news well. The look on her face, the calmness in her voice, and the stillness in her stance were shocking. It all changed during the walk home. Once again, I was reminded, "I am not taking care of any baby. I do not know what you are going to do, but you better figure it out."

I was used to figuring things out, but first I had to tell the father and hopefully together we would work it out.

Baby News

Now I had to not only tell this man I was pregnant, but I had to tell him the truth about my age and I was reluctant to do both. Standing outside my front door at the top of the steps blinded by the sun, I uttered these words to him, "I'm pregnant, and I lied to you about my age. I am only 15 years old."

This man looked at me with a shocked, nervous smirk and said, "I'm not 20; I am 23."

I was so worried about how he was going to handle the news about the pregnancy and my age. He definitely was not thrilled about my age and was concerned about how my mother was going to feel about his age, but it was too late; I was already pregnant. He wanted me to get an abortion and said he would pay for everything. I discussed that option with my mother and to my surprise she replied, "You are not getting rid of that baby. You laid down to make it, you will have it and take care of it."

I was feeling disappointed and that I made the biggest mistake of my life. After telling my mother his age she said, "You messed around and got pregnant by a grown ass man."

Things were just so complicated! We had to tell other family members about the pregnancy, which further made me want to crawl under a rock and never show my face again. *The judgment!* Although I was four months pregnant, I was not showing at the time. I was so embarrassed to be seen publicly.

I called my father to tell him I was pregnant, and he was not as upset as I thought he'd be, but he was disappointed. How mad could he really be at me; where was he throughout my life? I was just mad at the world.

To make matters worse, the father had been previously arrested on drug charges and was out on bail awaiting his court trial when we met—go figure. That was another part of his disclosure after I told him I was pregnant. He also said, "I have a court hearing coming up and I might be going to jail."

Which he later did. Now what? I knew nothing about him, I had seen his family maybe twice, and I am pregnant and left to take care of a baby alone without the father. My father was barely around in my life, and I did not want that for my child. Before he went to jail, he told his mother and sisters I was pregnant, and he told me to keep in touch with them. He would write me letters while in prison; in one of his letters, he asked me to name our son after him. I felt so alone. My mother made me responsible for everything, from making my appointments to finding my own way there by myself, which was walking most of the time.

Summer break was over, and it was time to return to high school pregnant in my sophomore year. I still was not noticeably showing, I had a little baby bump, but as time went on and my belly started to poke out more, questions about my pregnancy became overwhelming because there weren't a lot of teenage pregnancies during that time. I was ashamed of myself. My peers wanted to know how I got pregnant (not literally), and if the father was someone from the school. I wished it were then I would not have felt even worse being only 15 years old and pregnant by a grown man. I had no one to talk to who would really understand or could fix the problem.

I wanted to be happy about my baby, but would the excitement send the wrong message? What message was I trying to convey? *Do not be a teenage mom like me.* Was this the life I had created for myself? Fifteen and pregnant, what was I going to do with a baby?

I was happy that my mother started coming around and being more supportive of the pregnancy and me. She escorted me to a couple of my appointments and seemed to care about my and the baby's well-being. A pregnant teenager needs support in the midst of the difficult yet challenging situation as I was in. My mother's support gave me just that: a feeling of hope. No longer feeling isolated from a crowded world that existed right in front of me, I was ready to conquer the fears that were with me every day of becoming a first-time mom at 15, I had no choice.

My body was changing in drastic ways. I could not explain the tenderness of my breast and the milk that would leak from them. It was new to me. I shared some of my experiences with my mom when she was home and in the mood to listen. She would help me with some home remedies and encouragement about the reality of how pregnancy changes your body. Every day I watched this round bump in front of me and the growing human inside of my belly.

Appointments and prenatal care were pivotal; missing them was not an option. I made my way there no matter what, even alone and terrified. I still knew nothing about having a baby, pretending I understood what the doctor was saying about the progression of my pregnancy, mostly by nodding my head yes and not asking questions. When I was by myself, he'd ask, "Did you come alone?" and "Where is your mother?"

Yes, I came alone, and my mother is home. Even the couple times she came with me she would stay in the waiting room.

Baby on Board

It was a Sunday morning. This day seemed different. After taking my bath I needed to use the bathroom. I wiped myself and the tissue had something on it that I had never seen. "Ma, can you come into the bathroom?" I asked.

I showed her the tissue with the brown and light reddish jelly-like stuff. She was uncertain and made a phone call to Ms. M., the lady we used to live with; I believe she was a former nurse. I guess my mother forgot what it was like being pregnant. She described what was on the tissue and Ms. M. said it was my mucus plug and I was probably starting to dilate, and the baby would be on the way soon. I was afraid. The time was near, and I was about to become a teenage mommy.

Time was dragging along slowly and I became more anxious and uncomfortable. Lower back pain, constant urination, and an insurmountable amount of fear were clinging to me. I was pacing the hallway back and forth for hours, walking up and down the stairs, sitting and standing. On top of it all, I did not get any sleep. I was extremely exhausted. I had to be in labor!

Monday morning came and my mother decided it was time to take me to the hospital. Once I was examined, I was only at 2 centimeters and was released and told it should not be too much longer. I needed to be 4 centimeters dilated before they could keep me in the hospital. My mother and I went back home but as time continued to pass, the pain of labor became increasingly unbearable. I was uncomfortable, barely able to sit in one place. I started pacing the floor again, rubbing my lower back and walking. Finally, I could not take the pain any longer. My mother asked a neighbor for a ride to the hospital at around 5 a.m.

Once at the hospital, I was being prepped to deliver my baby. I was pretending to be strong, but nervous, and excited all at the same time. It was a cold winter Tuesday morning, February 9, 1988, and after five and a half hours of intense labor the most beautiful 5-pound, 16-ounce baby boy was born and placed in my arms.

If you could think of the most enjoyable moment in your life where you felt the happiest you have ever been, that was the highlight of my life. Time had stopped and I had this precious little gift that God blessed me with. I stared at my baby for what seemed like hours before the nurses took him from me. In an instant I was a mother now responsible for loving, supporting, nurturing, and protecting another human being that was birthed from my very own womb.

My son had a godmother who was two years older than me, and she loved my son just as much from the day she laid eyes on him. We became friends in high school; I think she had pity on me as a pregnant 15 year old and wanted to help me. I was in 10th grade and she was a senior with a job. She and her family were blessings in our lives and were heavily involved with taking care of my son.

I did tell my son's father's side of the family that I had the baby and they asked if I could bring him to see them when I was ready, and I agreed. His father only had about six months left in prison, and he could not wait to meet his only son (at least that is what he told me). My brother and sisters were also happy I had the baby, and a new addition was added to our family. They didn't quite understand what all the baby stuff really meant, but they knew their sister now had a baby in the home.

I was one month away from my 16th birthday and my days and nights were filled with sterilizing bottles, changing diapers, and a lack of sleep. I should have been planning my sweet 16 birthday bash, but instead I was on mommy-duty. I thought having my baby would make me feel better about myself, but I still felt defeated. I just could not seem to escape the staggering problems facing me every day. This new bundle of joy I had to care for and love with all my heart deserved my full attention, he was not responsible for my pain or the hurt that others caused… he was innocent. Having his godmother in our life made raising him a little easier, she helped me when I was unable to provide him with what he needed. I knew I would struggle leaving my baby after my maternity leave was over from school!

It was time to return to high school to finish 10th grade. My son was about 6 weeks old and my mother took on the responsibility of babysitting him while I attended school. I only had a few months left before school was over for the summer. I thought about my baby every minute I was away and could not wait to get home to cuddle with him. Loving him was easy. I still could not believe I had a baby.

One day, I came home from school to find my baby's diaper soaked with urine. My mother was high on drugs, and my baby boy was lying on the bed next to her. My mother's drug addiction was something I did not want to deal with after learning about it; I had gotten used to blocking it out, but I could not ignore it any longer. I was furious, but how was I going to approach this situation? I could not find the right words. She was definitely capable of taking care of my baby as she had many times. She'd never done this before, not sure why she was high during the time she was taking care of her grandson.

She wasn't doing drugs every day, but I never knew when she was going to. I was 16 years old with no job or money and could not afford daycare. I had no choice; she was my only child care resource and without her watching him I did not have a way to go to school. Tears rolled down my face as I changed my son's diaper saying to myself, *Why Lord?*

My mother was a functioning addict and at times she did not make the best decisions, especially when she was high. She loved us and cared for us, so I knew she could do the same with my baby and she did, mostly! I was simply left with trusting her to do the right thing.

Finally, it was the end of the school year, and I was ecstatic to be able to be with my baby all day. I just wanted him to be safe and I knew I was solely responsible for making that happen. Shortly after school was over, my mother said we had to move from the house we spent four years building stability. She did not pay the rent and we were going to be evicted; there was no way she could get the money in time. *What are we going to do? Where are we going to live?* My mother reached out to my aunt on my dad's side who lived in West Baltimore who said we could stay with her. She already had a full house because four of her six daughters were living with her at that time. How was that supposed to work?

Moving was not the same as before because I had a baby. We found ourselves cramped in one room: my mother, three siblings, my 4-month-old infant son, and me. Things would go from bad to worse for us. It was emotionally draining. Living with my aunt was not awful but I wanted a house of our own; it was not enough room for all of us. Staying with other people was exhausting—and I was sick of it!

My aunt's daughters (my cousin's) were allowed to do things I could not. Although I was a teenage mother, they were far more advanced and street smart then I had ever been. My aunt was more laid back in how she raised her daughters, they had no rules to follow and could be smart at the mouth at her, something I couldn't do with my mother. My cousin, who was the same age as me, lived with a man who could have been her grandfather. She was only 16 years old at the time. After about a month of us living with her mom she said to me, "You and your baby can move in with me." *Move with you where?* I thought. *You're a teenager like me, plus my mother would never allow that.*

She explained her living arrangements with this older man and it sounded appealing to me at the time. I wanted to take my baby and go, but my mother would have to agree, and I knew she would not. To my surprise, she said it was okay after I pitched the idea of moving with my cousin until we were able to get our own house. I couldn't figure out why this man, Mr. J, my cousin was living with would allow a 16-year-old girl and her baby move in. It was not long before I found out Mr. J liked young girls, and I became one that he loved.

It was summertime and I thought I was grown, living on my own. I was responsible for providing for my baby and myself with no job. My son's godmother was not thrilled with where and who I was living with and she wanted to get him more frequently so I would not have the responsibility alone. I thought it was a good idea, so I went along with it. I knew he was in good and capable hands, which gave me too much freedom. The days when I did not have my baby boy, I was out in the streets doing any and everything I thought I could do. My cousin introduced me to a world I didn't know existed, and I became entangled with men of all ages and I was losing my ability to control my sexual desires. Things only got worse.

CHAPTER 7

SPIRALING OUT OF CONTROL

(Nonstop Spinning)

Things don't spiral out of control when we surrender them; they spiral out of control when we try to control them!
—Marianne Williamson

Years of trauma had been suppressed and it was rearing its ugly head. I was becoming someone I never asked to be. Instead of confronting my issues, I removed myself further, pretending they did not exist. My cousin started teaching me how to act more like an adult and make money. I learned quickly how to follow in her footsteps. She had me doing stuff I never thought was possible and it was dangerous at times. My life took a turn down a path I wasn't certain I wanted to go down. I was a mother and my baby needed me, but the way I acted did not reflect that concern.

I was lost in my thoughts and stressed out as a teen, completely wiped out, I didn't know what to do. I spent many days and nights trying to figure it all out. I did not feel comfortable talking to anybody about my troubles, believing no one could possibly understand. I was afraid I was going to die in the streets before I could recover from my trauma. It was constant mental confusion and emotional chaos in my everyday life.

I wanted to talk to my mother about what had happened to me as a child with those relatives, but I was too ashamed to tell her and more afraid of her not believing me because of who they were. I could not risk the rejection.

Nothing was normal or simple for me. Everything seemed to blow up in my life. I was a ticking time bomb. My cousin continued to be a person who could only show me what I should not be doing and that was what I seemed to follow the most. I hated who I was. I had become completely mentally and emotionally disconnected from reality. Men were taking advantage of me with their sexual fantasies and desires. A part of me felt opened to the public like a house for sale, where men would tour me to see if I was worth buying. I was sleeping around all of the time like I was some sex addict. Older men found me to be more attractive than the boys my age did. After years of grown men forcing themselves on me sexually, being with older men seemed right or more comfortable to me. At that point, I would give my body away before any man could take it on their own. I wanted to feel I was a participating party in my sexual experiences, instead of a victim.

My trust had been violated as a child and I could not work through what happened. I did not feel safe by myself or in my own thoughts or around other people. With all the betrayal and abuse, I lost any purpose in my life outside of being a mother.

I was engaging in casual sex more frequently than I wanted to admit. Promiscuity was present in my life, traveling on the back of my heels. Everywhere I went some man was hitting on me, asking for my number or giving me theirs, and I was soaking it all in, responding to their needs. As if things could not get any worse for me, Mr. J, the man my cousin and I were living with, started making sexual advances toward me. *Here we go again, another old man wanting sex from a young girl.*

He could have been my grandfather, but how could I say no if I was going to continue living there? Mr. J. would tell me how pretty and smart I was and how he wanted to take care of my baby and I to provide a better life for us. He said I was different from my cousin, more mature and easier to talk to. I felt less than and dirty every time I had sex with him. I hated him touching me, kissing me, but I needed a place to live so I allowed it. I had become so detached from my feelings; I was damn near numb.

When I looked in the mirror, I did not like the person looking back at me. My body was tired, I was tired, but how could I turn off what my perpetrators had turned on before it was time to. I was so damaged, always feeling low and worthless, but I was on my own. Running away from it all sounded like a better plan. I cried out to God to help me, but He did not hear my cry.

One evening sitting alone, through my tears I thought back to the many times my mother's sister (my aunt) asked to raise my brother and I and my mom refused. *Why didn't my mother let me live with my aunt?*

I knew things would have been different for us, especially me. Very few people made me feel comfortable and safe after the sexual abuse, but one person that did was my aunt. I thought about memories of Christmas spent at her house every year since we were kids and how I was looking forward to it again. I wanted to call her and ask if my baby and I could live there, but I had too many problems and my aunt did not need the trouble. My life was in disarray, all out of whack and I felt like I had no control over what was happening.

Life was hard and it was only getting more difficult and challenging. The dysfunction all around was tearing me apart, ripping me into pieces. No one seemed to care, and I was left in this unpredictable world to handle all of the adult responsibilities on my own. Never knowing what to expect, but always feeling unprotected, neglected, and disregarded. My mother provided little to no support to me at this time and emotionally I felt I didn't matter and was unimportant. I learned how to function like everything was fine when nothing was. I survived in a world I knew, by not trusting or feeling, and numbing my pain with sex. I didn't know a healthy way to express myself, so I didn't and continued to bury the trauma deep inside. I was wounded and broken and everything bad going on in my life was my fault!

The Walls Came Tumbling Down

My baby was about 5 or 6 months old when his father came home from prison. I was happy he was home, so I did not have to feel like a single parent. Although, my son's godmother was very active in our life, being there for us every step of the way. My dad was not consistent in my life, but I wanted my child's father present in his to help raise him.

It was not long before his father started making demands and acting overly protective of the well-being of our son. He was ready to be a dad and spend as much time as he could with him, he even asked for our baby to live with him. He questioned my parenting and wanted to know why I was living with that old man. He clearly did not approve of my living arrangements, which I understood, but it was too soon to abruptly make the request to let my baby move in with him. He continued to press the issue, but I was not giving into his demands.

A couple of weeks later, he threatened to take me to court to take our son from me, calling me an unfit mother. I loved our child and there was no way I was going to let him take my baby. His godmother was prepared to help us get a lawyer if it went any further, this was not the welcome home I was expecting. After carefully considering his absurd and ridiculous actions he realized he only needed to worry about taking care of our son and staying out of my business, so he stopped threatening me. We co-parented as best we could afterwards, but I always kept an eye on him hoping we never had to revisit that conversation again. I had enough to figure out in my life, I did not need any added stress!

Summertime was coming to an end and school was about to start. What was I going to do with my baby? Figuring out my life was a never-ending story and needing someone to watch my baby was a great concern. My mother had moved from my aunt's house in West Baltimore and back in with the previous relative I did not want to live with or be around, especially not with my child. Plus, she was completely out of the way of where I would be going; how would I drop my baby off to her? My back was up against the wall, and it was time to start the 11th grade. At the last minute, my cousin offered to watch him, not because she wanted to, but I needed her to. I was only in school for a few weeks and had missed some days because my cousin was not reliable as a babysitter. Before long, dropping out of school was my only option. As if I did not have enough on my plate already, adding that to it made me feel more inadequate as a mom.

My mother asked me for weeks, "How was school today?"

She assumed my cousin was still watching my baby while I went to school because that's the story I told her. But after a while, she knew I was not being truthful. After I admitted to dropping out of school, my mother became so angry with me. She asked that I move into the home where she was living so she could re-enroll me back in school and watch my baby. I did not want to be in the company of my family, but I agreed, going against my better judgment, I was good at that. The thoughts of moving back with her were overwhelmingly stressful, but what other choice did I have? Once again, I had to pack our stuff and we moved from Mr. J and in with my mother.

I never wanted to be a high school dropout, but besides my cousin not always being available to babysit, I could not focus on school. There was simply too much going on in my life. My mind continued to wander all over the place thinking about life and all of its challenges. I was too young for all of this!

After moving in with my mother, I immediately regretted my

decision. I honestly was not fond of my family and that close proximity was a constant reminder of the abuse. I wanted to put everything about my past behind me, but how could I when I was connected to it every day. I knew what those relatives did was wrong, and I wanted to cut them off entirely, there was absolutely no trust, and I kept my baby close.

A couple of weeks after living there, I started to become involved in situations with different guys I had no business being with. I was meeting men all of the time. The city was flooded with them at every corner. Everywhere I went they knew I was a fresh, new face. "Hey shorty," "Hey beautiful," "Hey sexy," "Can I get your number?" is all I would hear.

I found myself loving the attention and taking it all in. I had fallen into a rabbit hole getting caught up in some strange and unlikely circumstances. I was blindly being exposed to some dangerous places that at times I was not sure I would make it out alive. When my son would be with either his father or godmother, it was like I did not care about myself and indulged in some risky behaviors with men. I was a young mother and my son deserved so much better than me. I wanted to change for him. I loved my baby so much, but I continued to make one bad decision after another. Maybe his father had every right calling me *unfit*.

Merry Go Round

I was close to becoming 17 years old and had been living back with my mother for a couple months when I met this man who I would soon be connected to forever. He was tall, dark, handsome, and a drug dealer—as well as an addict. He was on heroin. I would watch him sniff dope while we would be engaged in conversations and nod off right in the middle of talking. He was always so well dressed, taking much pride in his appearance. I did not judge his flaws; hell, I was drowning in all of my imperfections. His addiction did not affect me one bit; I would ignore it as if it was not happening in front of me. I had become used to my mother's addiction by that time, and this was no different.

We started out as friends and would talk about everything concerning our lives. I knew he had a girlfriend and a young daughter, but that did not deter us from getting involved with one another.

I knew he liked me, and not long after, I became his side chick. Although he was in a relationship, we would spend a lot of time together. He sold drugs in the neighborhood where I was living, so that gave me even more access to see him every day. He would make me feel like I was the most beautiful girl in the world, stroking my ego. He always made sure I had money and food; whatever I wanted, he made it happen. He started trusting me with more of his secrets as well as his drugs. I started holding his stash and getting him drug sales. The area where we lived was drug infested—it was easy to make money there. I never thought about the dangers of helping him sell drugs nor holding them. I mean, I was only selling a few pills here and there, and he would let me keep that money for myself.

One day, the house we were living in with my family got raided. The police came for me because they knew I was stashing his drugs in that house; I was under surveillance and did not know it. I heard them as they came in. I tried to hide the drugs in my underwear not knowing they would frisk me and find it, as they did.

"Tell us whose drugs they are! We know it's not yours, it's your boyfriend's. Tell us or you will lose your son and go to jail!" they said.

My mother was crying, holding my baby. "Monica, please tell them. Please!"

"It's mine," I continued to say.

THE UNVEILING

The police handcuffed me and took me to the police station. I was a scared teenager, but I did not show it. I was acting tougher than I actually was.

While at the police station, they begged me to stop protecting my boyfriend. They attempted to bust up his operation by getting me to tell on him. Their scare tactics to take my son away from me did not work. Later, I was released to my mom after hours of interrogation. My mother was so angry with me for not telling the police whose drugs they were. My boyfriend heard about what happened and how I did not snitch on him, and that made him love and trust me even more—at least that is what he said. He wanted to celebrate what was a victory for him at a hotel, and I believe that was the night I got pregnant.

A few weeks had passed and I was laying on the bed feeling nauseous, and suddenly I vomited. *Please God do not let me be pregnant!*

I went on as if that incident did not happen and was hoping I was not pregnant; there was no way I could have another baby. I kept what happened from him, there was no need to worry him about something that was probably nothing anyway. Besides, it was obviously an isolated incident because I only vomited that one time, it must have been something I ate!

One day, he and I had a big argument about his girlfriend. I was tired of being the side chick; he had to choose. I put him in a tough situation because he was not ready to make a choice, so I later broke it off with him. I was being selfish and so was he because he did not want me seeing other people, but he had a girlfriend. He pleaded for me not to leave him, but I did anyway. I really liked him, and I probably had some love for him too. It was difficult to fully connect with people I said I loved. I was having a tough time loving anyone completely; hell, I did not know how to love myself. I did not want to attach myself to anything I could not detach from, besides my baby. And it worked for me, I felt less clingy and tied to

92

people.

My mother and I agreed we needed to start looking for a place for us to move. We needed our own house and privacy, something we did not have there or anywhere when living with other people. Between my mother, my two sisters, my brother, my baby, me, and the people already living in that house, it was past time to move. Plus, it was hard for my mother on so many levels being in direct contact with the drugs she was trying to stay away from. On top of that, it was impossible to keep staying with a family I was not fond of. Once we began our search for a house we found this nice, affordable three-bedroom house that was perfect for us. We could not wait to move into our own home and get away from that toxic environment. All I prayed for was that we stayed in the next house a little while longer. Each time we moved, I worried because I never knew just how long we 'd be settled in one place!

We were in our home for about a month or so before I noticed something was not right with my body—I was tired all of the time and craving certain foods. Immediately, I thought back to when I had that vomiting episode. *Oh dear God! My mother is going to kill me. I just turned 17 years old; I cannot be a teen mother again! This cannot be happening right now!*

I needed to know if I was pregnant, clearly I was not paying attention to my monthly cycle.

I soon found out after taking a pregnancy test that I was indeed pregnant. *What am I going to do? I cannot have this baby!*

I called my cousin telling her how I was pregnant and could not have another baby and that I was going to get an abortion. That was my only option. I was a nervous wreck; my mother cannot know about this. She advised against it. She understood my concerns, but she tried to encourage me to rethink my decision. I was not sure she understood how complicated this situation was and how much of an emotional toll it was to think about caring for another child.

How in God's name could this be happening to me right now?

After carefully considering what my cousin said, I guess keeping the baby was the right thing to do… but it was a tough choice. I had to tell my mother and I knew she would blow a gasket. I was feeling panicky and on my own, I just wanted her emotional support!

"Ma, I am pregnant again."

"What? Oh no, you're getting out of here. I am not raising any more kids—this child you have is still in diapers! Your hot ass messed around and got pregnant again."

I was so hurt and wanted to run away to escape her harsh words. My mother did not believe in abortions, and I needed her consent since I was under the age of 18.

I decided I would give my baby up for adoption. It was one of the hardest decisions to make, but it was for the best. I did not want the father to know I was pregnant so I kept it a secret from him until I couldn't any longer. I pondered daily on the idea of putting my baby up for adoption. It broke my heart!

One day, the father came to my house unannounced asking if I was pregnant and I said, "No. Why would you ask me that?"

He'd found out from one of my family members that my brother told. He said, "Just tell me the truth."

So, finally I confessed. I was not showing—you could barely tell I was pregnant although I was a few months along. I told him I was giving the baby up for adoption and he asked me not to, but I did not care. My mind was made up. It was my decision, and it was final.

My mother was angry about the pregnancy, but she was not in agreement with me giving my baby away. Life for me had already changed with having one baby, let alone two. There was no way I could financially support another child. This would be too stressful, and I was not prepared to take on this challenge. Every day I became more concerned about my decision to give my baby up for adoption. I later found out I was having another boy and I tried my best to not connect with the human growing inside of me because I knew he was not coming home with me. I had to keep the promise I made to myself to go back to school and having another baby would only interfere. I tried to think of a way to make it work, but there was no logical way. I hoped my baby would be raised in a loving home with a good family. My life would be forever changed, and my heart was being broken in half. I questioned what type of person I would be to give away my own child! *God please forgive me!*

The father would call to see how I was doing and if I changed my mind. It was difficult to explain to him why I was going to put our baby up for adoption. The decision was very emotional and I had such conflicting feelings, those thoughts continued to linger but I did not see any other way. The closer it got to my delivery date, the more anxious I was becoming. I wasn't convinced I was making the right decision, oh Lord help me. I just wanted everybody to leave me alone and give me space to breathe!

Baby No. 2

The time was near. I began to feel discomfort and I knew it would not be long before the baby would be born. The day dragged along slowly but the lower back pain was excruciating. I walked around my block several times to try to ease the delivery process. The more I walked, the more pressure I felt, and I knew the baby was ready to enter into the world. I told my mother it was time. She was not able to go with me to the hospital because she had to take care of my first son, but she had a neighbor drive me instead. I was by myself, but I was okay. I was at the hospital on the night of September 17,1989, for about four-to-five hours before it was time to deliver.

After pushing out my 7-pound, 8-ounce baby boy and seeing his cute face with those chubby cheeks and thick hair, how could I not want to keep him? I cried at the thought of leaving him in the hospital and going home empty-handed; I could not do it. Instantly I fell in love with him. My mother did eventually arrive, and I told her I did not want to give my baby away. She agreed and knew I had made the right decision.

Now what? Once I realized he was coming home we had to think of a plan fast. *What would I call him?* He needs clothes, diapers, everything—I was not prepared. My cousin gave him his first name, and I gave him his father's middle name and my last name. The naming part was easy. My mother called a relative who she knew had a son and could probably help out with clothes, as his child was no longer an infant. He had a lot of baby clothes that he gave us. My mother's boyfriend bought Pampers, wipes, and milk. All of sudden we had what we needed to come home. The father was informed of my decision to keep the baby, not that his feelings mattered one way or another, but he deserved to know our son was coming home. Although, he did come to the hospital the next day to see the baby and that was enough for me. I did not want anything else from him. I had a sudden shift in my thinking after choosing to keep my baby. It was time for me to change and pull myself together for my children!

It was tough being a teenage mom of two babies, but I did my best to care for them. My first son's godmother and his father provided what he needed, which took some of the load off of me. I was 17 with two children and I was left to think about where my life was headed. The hardest part was trying to balance raising my two babies, along with other responsibilities that were not my own. While making my decisions I did not consider the impact it would have on my day-to-day life. My life no longer belonged to me; from then on I had to live for my children and do what was in their best interest. But I was not certain of how to always do that. I found myself questioning everything and wanting to be this amazing mother for them. I wanted to be intentional about how I loved them and whom I allowed around them. One thing for sure, nothing was the same and I was constantly learning how to be a single mother.

Although my mother was not over the hill about me now having two children, I told her I wanted to go back to school as I promised I would. She was excited about my decision, and so was I, it was extremely important for me. A month after my son was born, I enrolled back into school. It was long overdue, but never too late. I had enough credits that I was able to start 12th grade. I started changing my ways and being more focused on raising my kids and getting my high school diploma. My mother watched my babies while I went to school. I went to school half the day and work release the other half at Johns Hopkins hospital in their medical records department as a student, which was part of my credits to graduate. Life was beginning to look positive for me.

I was getting good grades and staying on top of my schoolwork making sure I did not fall behind. Being a young mom while trying to complete high school was difficult for me, but I knew I had to finish if not for me, then for my children. Providing a better life for them meant everything to me, therefore I continued to push myself all the more. I was determined to beat the odds and navigate through the difficulties of teen motherhood. The motivation to earn my high school diploma was ever so close.

Planning and preparing for prom night could not have felt better. I could not believe it was happening, but it was, and it was an unexplainable excitement. Shopping for my dress and shoes, getting my hair done, and taking my brother as my date was everything that made it great. The best part was the feeling of accomplishing what I had only hoped for. Some might not care about their prom, but not me. I needed to have that experience as part of my process. That night meant more than dressing up, dancing, pictures, and mingling with my classmates; it was purposeful and meaningful. After all the darkness in my life, this light shined so bright and it was undeniably one of the best nights of my life. I did not know what the future would look like for me, but graduation was the next step. I was going to make something out of my life!

It was getting closer to the time for graduation. I reflected on the obstacles that made the upcoming day even more profoundly amazing. I did not want the stigma attached to me of being a teenage, single mom and high school dropout on welfare. The determination I developed was far beyond my fears of failing. I changed myself for the better to make it to graduation day. I was not going to let anything stand in the way of that not happening.

I did it! I was 18 years old with a 2-year-old and 9-month-old son walking across the stage to receive my high school diploma. My mother was so proud of me, as was I. A day of gratitude, tears, and opportunities! My diploma was more meaningful in my life than my childhood dream of becoming Michael Jackson.

I went from being a student employee to being offered a full-time position at Johns Hopkins and I kindly accepted. A real job with benefits, now I can really take care of my children! Everything seemed to be going in the right direction and it was time for the next accomplishment. I decided I was going to learn how to drive and get my license, and so I did. I was determined to be somebody in a world that labeled teen pregnancy as a failure. The weight of motherhood was heavy on my shoulders, but I carried it with resilience and perseverance as best I could. I knew there would be more challenges ahead of me, but giving up now was not an option. I had made too much progress.

Me at 16 with my first born son.

I was sixteen years old trying to figure it out.

I was so lost at 16 with no direction in life.

Just trying to find love, 16 and confused.

My first born son around 1-2 months old.

CHAPTER 8

My Life Turned Inside Out

(Fight or Flight)

*Why not touch things that we hate and turn them upside
down and inside out.*
—Alber Elbaz

Despite the excitement of graduating from high school and getting offered a job, there were things still looming in the shadows. My personal life was complicated, and I could not catch a mental break. Little did I know that I would come face to face with the abuse I had suffered from. There were times I felt I was over it and living my life as best as could despite the sexual abuse.

I had responsibilities to take care of, like my family and children. Although my brother was a year younger than I was he never had to stepped up as I did. He looked out for himself and the streets had already had their hooks in him and trouble followed him early on in life. The court system, detention centers, and jail had a space with his name on it. At times, I was afraid the cemetery did too. I did not talk much to him about how deeply affected I was over the abuse, unfortunately, he wouldn't have understood the way I needed him to.

I was the oldest of my siblings; there was an expectation for me to fix all of the problems. They looked up to me, as did my mother, especially once I started working. Things were becoming stressful and bills were piling up and I had my shared portion to pay. My paychecks I was bringing home was not enough to cover and pay for all my expenses.

I tried to turn a new leaf, but I seemed to be faced with problems that resorted to me needing a man for something. I knew how to get money when I found myself in a financial bind. I was telling myself not to sleep around for money, but everything was piling up on me. Maya Angelou said, "Do the best you can until you know better. Then when you know better, do better."

This did not apply to me; I only knew what I had always done, or what was always done to me. I wanted to have other options. I wanted to know something different so I could do better. I thought I was making a fresh start but somehow, I was knocked backward. I was not ready to confront my fears or all the reasons I continued to give in to these men? I wanted to close the door on them, lock it, and throw away the key, but I always gave a man his way that was all I knew.

Some men were taking care of me financially while a few did nothing but say, "Thank you for a good time."

I did not want to use my body for money, but I had so many responsibilities and I could not handle them alone. Finding myself in those situations was when I thought about my father the most. I did not want to blame him for my choices, but I believed his absence, outside of the sexual abuse, was the cause of my problems in life. I felt hopeless and empty!

The Reality of My Pain

I used my body to get what I wanted and what I thought I needed, although I hated it every time because it made me feel cheap and nasty. My body always said I was ready; it was prepared for any and everything. My body always called the ones that did not deserve me, it always told them I wanted something I did not need. My body was always in disguise prepared to do things I could never wash away. It never told the truth; it lied to men making them believe I was feeling good all the while I was disgusted. I told them what they needed to hear. The whispers in their ears, the moans and groans that boosted their ego made them stroke me harder, grab me tighter, and squeeze me longer. I became bitter, angry, and resentful as I complied with their demands, feeling lower than a prostitute on the corner. I felt shameful, but it did not stop me from doing it again. I didn't deserve to be loved, but I wanted to, however, I lost that feeling a long time ago. There were many nights I wanted to just hide from myself, the shame, guilt, and secrets were heavy loads to carry. It was hard to understand my own feelings. I could not explain it!

I was a good mother to my children, taking care of and loving them completely, but I had no self-respect or self-worth for myself. I was wrapped up in the arms and beds of men all of the time; I was defined by my performance in the bedroom. My worth was about how much sex I was having, love had nothing to do with it. I wanted to be more than a sex object, but I was damaged goods and beyond repair. Laying on my back was the only thing I was good for—at least that's what I believed. I wanted to be happy that I had earned my diploma, had a decent job and two beautiful sons. But I could not seem to put what happened to me as a kid behind me, mostly because I was left to still face the relative who first abused me, he mattered more than the others as his abuse was for years of my life.

I wished I could've enjoyed being a little girl, but instead I had been sexually abused by several men from age 7 until I was 16 years old. It caused so much confusion and years of finding myself naked and ashamed. I was just a kid who ended up having kids, because I was always on a sexual high chasing after my drug of choice—sex and men. My self-esteem was being flushed down the toilet after every sexual encounter no matter how good it felt. By this time in my life nothing felt meaningful or worthwhile, but my children. Everything that would have matter to me was taken away the moment he kissed my lips. He or the others never knew the emotional damaged they caused nor did they care. During my teenage years, my sense of value was destroyed, I wasn't liking myself and I was my worst enemy.

I had experienced the type of trauma no child should ever have to. The hurt I was feeling was different, I was sick carrying around their filthy dirty secrets. Nobody was taking responsibility for the years of abuse and betrayal they caused. Somehow, I had to shake it off, way in the back of mind I knew I had to move on in my life, I now had two children and because of them life wasn't so bad. They loved me and I loved them back, my sons were more important and they were my pride and joy. I had to tucked away the pain, life had more to offer me. By no means did trying to move on replaced the trauma and change my view of the perpetrators.

The Yes That Should Have Been No

One day, my brother's girlfriend asked me if I could take her to pick her daughter up from the father and I agreed. I did not have my own car, but my mother's boyfriend would often let me drive his truck if I had something to do. Once we arrived to meet her daughter's father, as he was putting the baby in the car, we locked eyes and spoke—*yeah, he was cute.*

The very next day my brother's girlfriend called me saying, "Guess who likes you?"

"Umm who?"

"My ex."

"What, really?"

"He wants me to give you his number."

I knew that was a bad idea, but I took the number and called anyway. "Hey sexy," he said.

That's all it took to put a smile on my face, and I wanted to hear more. I think it was the way he said it. I was used to hearing compliments, but during our entire conversation he was flattering with his words. I am sure he used that charm on plenty of girls, but somehow I fell for it.

I asked my brother's girlfriend if she was sure she was okay with us talking, and she assured me that she was. They were only good friends, and he was just the father of her child. Again, I knew it was a bad idea, but he said I was beautiful, fine, and sexy... silly me. How many times did I need to fall for words before seeing any action? The problem was I did not know what to look for or expect in a man.

We talked every day for about a week, and we were dying to see each other, so I went over to visit him at his mother's house where he lived. He was waiting for me at the door and greeted me with a big smile and hug. He was tall and skinny, and I thought he was cute with a baby-looking face. He was only 18 and I had just turned 19, but he was only a month or so from turning 19 himself. I was used to older men, but I gave him a chance. We sat on the couch and talked and shortly after we started kissing, which led to my pants being pulled down and having sex. I knew after it was over that I would be pregnant, we didn't use any protection. *Damn not again.*

I was falling in love with him. He was so charming and seemed to be into me. *Was I fooling myself?* We continued to talk every day afterward and saw each other as often as we could. Then he finally asked me to be his girlfriend and I gladly accepted. I felt like I was checking a YES, NO, or MAYBE SO box like back in my middle school days!

Not long into our relationship, I found out I was pregnant after missing my menstrual cycle that month. I barely knew him and now I would be the mother of his child, my third baby daddy. So many thoughts were running through my mind, I did not know how I would provide for yet another child when I was barely making it with the two I had. I was working but adding another baby expense to my budget would be overwhelming.

It was time to tell him about the baby—*what would he say, how would he respond, would he want this child*? He already had a 6-month-old daughter, but he had to know. Here we go again. Why did I continue to find myself in these situations?

I'm pregnant. To my surprise he was more excited than I was, smiling ear to ear. I was not expecting that response. We were just too young to have all these kids, my two, his one and soon another.

Now the hardest part was telling my mother again that I was pregnant with yet another baby. I was already living in her home in a room with my 3- and 2-year-old children—now a third child? This was not going to go over well, and it did not. I was told I needed to leave and get my own place because another child was too much. Although I was an adult and was working to provide for my children, she was right. We already had a house full, and my children and I slept in a bed together; it was pretty crowded.

The life of being pregnant again—doctor's appointments, and eating everything not nailed down—was soon going to be my reality. I was excited to finally have a baby with someone who was happy to become a daddy though. But the saying, "All good things come to an end," reared its ugly head right before my eyes.

All I wanted was to finally be happy and in a committed relationship with someone who loved me as much as I loved them; was that too much to ask? For me it was.

Desperate for Love

After a couple months of dating, our relationship hit a few rough patches, nothing I could not handle. We were still getting to know one another, and it was not easy. There were things happening that were questionable, but we would talk about them and move on. Our time together was becoming more bittersweet due to some trust issues. I thought he would be everything I needed in a relationship, but it turned out he was just like the others. As much as I tried to ignore the early warning signs because I wanted to love him so badly, I could no longer turn the other cheek. It was intensely difficult finding out he was cheating. My life always had a way of being turned inside out. Then again, it was no surprise something like this would happen.

I was only a few weeks pregnant, and I asked myself the question, *Do you want this drama in your life?*

After much consideration it was not worth it. I did not want to have a baby with him anymore. It was not the best decision, but I felt it was for me. I made the appointment to abort our child.

He was not in agreement, but I did not need, nor did I want a third child with another man I could not trust. He tried to deny the cheating, but the evidence was there. He was sleeping around behind my back and what made matters worse was his refusal to admit the truth. I was so angry with him! *I knew it was a bad idea from the beginning!*

Our relationship was becoming more and more toxic, which validated my decision not to keep the baby. My appointment was one day away, and I'd been having mixed feelings about having an abortion, but it was necessary. Monday morning with $250, my best friend, and my nerves, I headed to Planned Parenthood. *Am I doing the right thing, will I regret this decision, how will I live with myself*—all the thoughts running through my mind.

Walking into that clinic shaking like a leaf, I was terrified. Too late to turn back now! *It is time, they are calling my name.* Walking back to the exam room to undress and put the gown on to be checked before my procedure, I wanted to run in the opposite direction.

"The doctor will be with you shortly."

I laid on the table with my eyes filled with tears, wondering who and what I was killing. The doctor came in to do his examination, and what came next was surprising: "I'm sorry, you will need to come back in about two weeks. You need to be further along in your pregnancy."

Wait what? I was instructed to get dressed and go to the front desk to make an appointment for two weeks from that day. Puzzled of course, I did what I was told and was given back my money for my next scheduled date.

Once I arrived back home, I called my boyfriend to tell him what happened and he was happy, hoping that I would reconsider my decision. I never told my mother I was getting an abortion, so I did not have to explain anything to her. I had enough to ponder!

I could not stop thinking about what happened while waiting those two dreadful weeks. Every day I went back and forth. *Should I keep my baby or not?* I was not feeling right about the abortion; too much time to think about it.

But then it was the weekend, a few days before I had to go back to the clinic. Obviously, even at work it appeared that I was bothered by something because on a Sunday evening my phone rang, and it was my coworker. She was concerned about me and wanted to see if she could help me in any way. I shared with her about my most challenging decision that was less than 24 hours away. After hours of a thought-provoking and encouraging conversation, I was left uncertain of my choice to abort my baby. After a sleepless night, Monday morning arrived and I made the phone call, "Hello, my name is…and I want to cancel my appointment."

Did I make the right choice? I called the father to tell him the news; he was so excited, but I was not. I was not sure how to feel, but I needed to start my prenatal care. He seemed to be smitten with the idea of becoming a father again, but his mom not so much. She felt like we were both too young to have another baby. She reminded us both of the children we already had and the expense of kids as if we did not know that, but I understood what she was telling us. After a while she got on board with the idea of us having a baby and it being our choice to do so.

I tried to be happy with the idea of carrying another life inside of my body, but I could not feel the joys of motherhood. The baby's father and I were not getting along; we were barely keeping it together, holding on by a string. Several months into my pregnancy I found out I was having another boy, which made me even unhappier. A third son… I wanted a daughter! I was going through so much, and my hormones were all over the place. It was just too much. I wanted to break free from him and everything connected to him so badly, but I did not want to have another baby without being with the father. I tried to make it work after countless apologies and "I will never do it again."

It was causing me too much anxiety. I did not want to break up but there were more women he was cheating on me with as if the others were not enough. Now I was pregnant, stressed, and hated my life. I was feeling unloved.

How could he do this to me? I loved him and it finally felt good to be with one man who I believed loved me. I began to regret my decision to keep his baby; I started to despise my pregnancy and I wanted the baby gone. I did not allow myself to connect emotionally to my baby because of the pain the dad was causing me. I did not know how to separate the two. This innocent baby growing inside of me could not feel the love of his mother. I would break up with the father only to accept him back over and over again more times than I should have. He was causing so much stress on my body that I had to get a stress test done two times a week to monitor the well-being of the baby and to make sure he was getting enough oxygen.

To make matters even more complicated, I found out he was using drugs again. Even though I was privy to his history with drugs when we met, he told me he was no longer using. My life was turning upside down and I was experiencing an emotion I had never felt before. I was so in love with him I could not make a rational and stern decision to stay away from him. I allowed this man to emotionally and mentally drain me with his lies and deception. I was tired of the waterfall of tears, but I loved him and wanted to believe his "I'm sorry." Was he really sorry? No! He misused my love for him and took advantage of my heart.

My stress tests were every Tuesday and Friday, and with everything he was putting me through, I never knew what the results of my test would be. When I would have these uncertain feelings about men, I wanted to talk to my father about them. We were not in constant communication, but we did occasionally speak. He was not thrilled about me having a third baby; that opinion did not matter to me. I wanted him to know the type of men I continued to attract, hoping he would have an epiphany. Nope, not him! I said to myself, *"Daddy you are the reason I keep picking shitty men."*

I stayed with my boyfriend, but nothing really changed, and I worried myself sick. Right before Christmas, I was told I had to be on bed rest until my due date or further notice. My due date was scheduled for February 14, but the stress my body was experiencing caused my baby to come early. I went in on a Tuesday for my test only to be told I needed to be induced immediately because I had little-to-no amniotic fluids and the baby had to come out that day. The doctor told me he was not sure how the baby survived and there would be a possibility he'd be taken to the neonatal intensive care unit (NICU) as soon as he was born. At that very moment I loved my baby so much and wanted him to be okay. I could not stop crying and thinking about all the awful things I felt about him. *Please let my baby be healthy.*

After 12 long hours of labor, on January 21, 1992, at 11:57 p.m. my 7-pound, 6-ounce, healthy baby boy was born without any complications. I looked into his beautiful brown eyes and knew he was a precious miracle from God! His father was with me during delivery, but my feelings had not changed, I was still on the fence about our rocky relationship. After two days in the hospital, it was time to take my little one home, but what about the father of my baby? I needed to let him go; I wanted him out of my life. He had become a stressor I no longer could give attention to. I wanted to focus on being a new mom again and possibly raising another child without the other parent. He wanted to be a family, but there was no trust, it had been broken too many times.

Never want something so bad that you are willing to sacrifice your peace.

He promised he would get himself together and more importantly stop using drugs, and as usual, I gave my boyfriend another opportunity to prove himself to me, going against my better judgment. I had been used and abused so long, honestly this felt no different. My mind had become programmed to accept the unacceptable and to be comfortable with the uncomfortable. One night, my two sons and I laid in my bed with the baby in his bassinet and tears running down my face, as I prayed for a better life. I wanted so badly for him to love us and to make it alright, but I was not sure he could give us the real love we deserved. Sometimes what we want the most is not at all what we need. I'll admit it, I really wanted to keep him around in my life. I did not want to be alone, and I really did love him.

He had hurt me more times than I could count, but somehow, I found a way to trust him again. Honestly, I had so many mixed emotions that I had not quite figured out yet, but one thing for sure he was the only one of my child's fathers who stayed with me.

THE UNVEILING

Maybe I was holding on to us one day being a real happy family, something I never had with the other two fathers. No matter how bad things would get between us, he never wanted to leave me or never walked away, although he was the one causing the discord.

After all the back and forth with my son's father, I was still uncertain of a future with him, however, I was still dreaming of the life we could have together. Love is not always going to be perfect, and some things are just meant to be, so taking another chance with him was one I hoped was not another mistake. There goes my heart being handed over to him again, hoping he would love me right that time.

We decided we would move in together; I was thinking this would solidify our family and our love. I was worried, but I did not want it to stop us from moving forward in our already rocky relationship. Despite all of the cheating, it was not an easy thing to heal from. However, I was willing to repair the relationship. He seemed remorseful, but he always did; maybe this time he felt deeply sorry. I was just tired of second guessing my relationship and now the move. At the end of the day I had to believe our love for one another would get us through the rough patches. Living together was going to either strengthen or break us, but we were willing to take that chance. After finding what we thought was a perfect two-bedroom apartment, it was really time we moved on with our life. No turning back now, this was a big step for the both of us, being as though neither of us had ever lived on our own.

I was 17 and pregnant with son number 2.

Me and my second son.

Senior portraits 1990.

1990 year I'll never forget.

Senior Prom with my brother as my date 1990.

My two babies.

THE UNVEILING

CHAPTER 9

TURNING IT AROUND

(The Waves Of Life)

***No Matter How Far You Go In The Wrong Direction,
There's Always A Chance To Turn Your Life Around.
—Kushandwizdom***

I had gone through so many ups and downs and all I wanted was something solid and real in my life. Despite it all, I must say, I was so excited to be in my apartment because I finally felt a sense of stability, and hopefully, I'd have a peace of mind. I never had time to just stop and think about my own life, because I was always taking care of everybody else's. So working, paying bills, and taking care of just my family felt good. Yes, it was a pleasure walking through the front door of what I called home. My relationship with my boyfriend was not the best, but we were still together.

I was hoping things would get better with my boyfriend, but he was still showing signs that made me doubt he could provide for our family and be faithful to me. He was working odd jobs here and there, and seemed satisfied with that. He paid bills when he could, making it more of my responsibility to keep a roof over our heads. He needed to do better with his life, but I was not sure if he wanted to. Why was I settling for this man? I wanted to be loved and accepted as the woman I thought I was becoming for him. No matter how hard I tried to make what was wrong right, it failed. I was grown; I did not have time to play house and childish games. I was doing all the right things for the wrong person, and nothing was ever good enough. I thought we were going in a better direction that would strengthen our relationship, but I was not feeling the love, or maybe he was not. Either way it was not working. I just wanted to enjoy my home, that's all.

After a couple of months being in our apartment, and what do you know? A knock at the door; it's my mom and two sisters. I was happy to see them but the looks on their faces were not pleasant but that of distress. My mom asked if I could come out so she could talk to me. *I wonder what this could be about.*

"Can we stay with you?"

There goes that little girl (me) responding with a yes, too afraid to say no. She began telling me that she could no longer stay with my stepfather because it was not working out; they were miserable there. I realized I said yes without talking it over with my boyfriend. I told my mom to give me a minute, I needed to let him know what was going on. I noticed they had their bags in the car of the person who drove them to my place—she knew I would say yes. After talking with him he was not happy about my mom and two sisters moving into our two-bedroom apartment, but he said, "It's your mom, I guess she can stay if she has no other options."

Have you ever felt that what you thought was a good idea could turn into a nightmare?

I Never Saw It Coming

Two weeks in and I said to myself, *okay, this is not as bad as I thought it would be.* Coming home from work with dinner cooked and the house cleaned made me happy. It was the little things that mattered. Our apartment was just enough for the five of us, however I convinced myself there was more than enough space for the eight of us. Unconsciously, I knew deep inside I made a mistake, but they needed me and I was not going to let them down. I loved my family even though we did not always get along or agree.

I knew my mom struggled with drugs, but I prayed she would not do drugs while living with us, but I knew that was wishful thinking. Although she was not showing any present signs of drug use, I'm sure that was a potential reason she did not want to stay living with stepfather. She did not use drugs every day and I was hoping she would stay clean, not just for a couple of months, but forever. I had learned to cope with her addiction, but it was always hard to live with. I had to grapple with the idea that I had a functioning drug-addicted mother who at times would go on her drug binges.

One night, she did exactly what I hoped she would not do and that was leave to go get high. I was so disappointed. We did not know where she was, but we knew she was in one of those houses where she would go to do drugs. She never liked me coming to look for her at the drug houses, and that time I did not. My youngest sister who was about 10 at the time would cry for our mother. I would tell her, "Do not cry, she will be back."

My other sister who was almost 16 was rebellious, doing her own thing and not listening or following my or my mother's rules.

Eventually, my mother did come back after a couple of days but not without problems. She was tired, exhausted, guilt-ridden, crying, and hungry, but I was used to that. No matter how upset I was, we were just glad she was home. It was time for me to help replenish her making sure she ate, drank plenty of fluids, and rested. But soon after being back she complained of her arm hurting. It was not getting better, only worse. Later, we learned that while on her binge she shared a drug needle. Her arm looked infected, and she had to be taken to the hospital. I was no doctor, but I knew something was wrong, and surely, I was right. She had an infection. My mom had to get an emergency procedure on her arm and the infection had to be drained, and her wound had to be packed with gauze and bandaged. I'm not good with blood and I knew I was not going to be responsible for changing her bandage, but somebody had to. My youngest sister took the job and nursed our mother's arm, changing the bandages daily. I tried not to believe she cared more about the drugs than her own children, but her disappearing for days at a time made that impossible.

I was becoming exhausted. My relationship wasn't the best, but I was neglecting my boyfriend more and more. This move was starting to wear me out and worrying about my mother did not help matters. What happened to my safe haven and my peace? Everything around me was falling apart and I did not know how I was going to deal with all the stressors; I wanted to escape. My children were unaware of the chaos, they were too young to understand and God knows I wanted to keep it that way. I was responsible for their well-being, my siblings, mom, and my boyfriend that I did not want to give up on. I loved him. He was complaining all the time about our life and was gone away from the home more frequently. I was hoping he did not relapse on drugs—maybe he just wanted to get away from my family. I tried to be understanding of his feelings and cater a little more to him. I wanted to strengthen our relationship in a way I thought would help us. "Do you want to start going back to church?" I asked him, and he agreed.

I thought church was the answer and would make all of our problems go away. We enjoyed our time at church and Bible study. I thought we were getting closer because of it. I would come home and would just bask in the peace of God, making every effort to ignore everything around me that could easily agitate me. I did not want anything to disrupt the change I was attempting to make. We would take my little sister to church with us sometimes too.

In July 1992, we decided to get baptized. It was an amazing feeling to go through a life changing experience with the man I loved; surely, this would change us for the better. My mom and rebellious sister were still not getting along and at times I had to step in between the two of them. But I was doing my best to manage my new relationship with the Lord. Finally, I was getting my family back on track, so I thought, but I couldn't say for sure because my boyfriend missed a couple Sundays at church with the kids and me.

Was I Expecting Too Much?

Women know when something is wrong, we can feel it. I had been feeling it but did not want to believe it because God was in our lives and we, or so I thought, were changing. I found out my boyfriend was cheating and using drugs again. How did I miss the signs, or did I just turn a blind eye and deaf ear to the truth? I was crushed so I put him out of the house, even though my heart wanted him to stay. I had been through so much already with him and was so in tuned with caring about his feelings that I had suppressed my own. In doing so, I essentially overlooked what was crystal clear—he was not willing to change.

So many thoughts began to resurface. I started thinking back to a time when I came home early from work and the smell of sex was in my bedroom and I knew it was not from me. Thinking back on the lies he told me repeatedly about not getting high, making me believe I was delusional. I chose to ignore all of the signs of infidelity and addiction that were in my face. I would question him about so many things, and of course, he made me believe I was crazy and denied everything. How did we get here again or were we here all along?

I noticed my mom wasn't upset about the breakup. Actually, she was relieved he was gone. But why? I guess she saw the grief he was causing me. We did have a child together, so I could not cut him out of my life completely, although I wanted too. In addition to ignoring all the obvious signs, I could not deny how in love I was with this man-child who was refusing to get his life together. Even though he caused incredible pain in my life, I knew him, and I had learned how to function in the dysfunction with him. He was

119

dragging me along in the only world he knew, and we lived in what was familiar to the both of us. We were comfortably uncomfortable with each other and therefore, the breakup did not last long. After many conversations, I allowed his tears, manipulation, and "I am sorry" to cause me to give him another chance, once again. We decided to start over, go on dates, and get another place to stay once the lease was up a few months later. Although we were back together, we thought it would be best if he did not move back in the apartment. Things were never the same for us once my family moved in anyway.

He would come over and stay some nights and I saw him at his mother's house too. It was not easy being back together because the trust was definitely questionable. As much as I tried to rebuild the trust, I knew it would take time and patience–something I was not motivated to do during the times when I thought about the betrayal. I was afraid of getting hurt again, his track record made it difficult for me to trust him again. Instead, I acted accordingly this time. What came out of his mouth and what I was feeling was not the same, I did not want to be let down again, but I expected to be... I was losing control of my logic.

Unfortunately, given our trust and history together, it was becoming so hard for me to put aside my doubts. He was trying to get me to believe in him, but it was not enough because I had already caught him in little white lies and that sabotaged the trust. Soon after, my thoughts proved to be accurate, I found out my boyfriend had not changed as much as he said he did and was still seeing other women. My life was in shambles, and I did not know what to do to make it better. I had enough of excusing, overlooking things he was doing, and forgiving the same person who could not commit to his word, let alone me. I did not trust myself, my decisions, my family, and I even started doubting God. I told myself there was no good in the world and it was a waste of time trying to be perfect, it did not exist.

I wish I'd never answered the door that night when my mother knocked. Everything that could go wrong seemed to have done so. My life was blowing up in my face and nobody was taking responsibility for their part in the mess. I wanted to blame my family moving in with us for the problems we were having so it would make sense. But he was not ready to change and I could not make him either and my family did not cause him to lie or cheat that was his own doing.

Wondering why I continued to place myself in the same situations with someone who treated me so badly? It's so obvious! I had not seen a healthy relationship, therefore creating one was nearly impossible. On the other hand, this was with a man I thought loved me, making it easier for me to be vulnerable and weak for him.

Not being properly loved by my father created a sense of neediness. I was seeking approval and attention from my boyfriend that my father failed to provide. My worth was based on him validating me, which I craved making me emotionally needy for his love and reassurance—something he himself lacked. I was a single mother of three sons and I wanted him to be the male figure in their lives.

The problem is that I was expecting a man-child to figure out how to father boys and love me at the same damn time. Did I put too much pressure on him to actually provide and take care of a family of five? And to be responsible for leading us when he was lost?

With everything going on and trying to figure out my life, I still had to parent and love my three children who did not ask to be involved in that mess. As innocent as they were, I knew they felt the constant tension around them. Surprisingly, when he was not at the house the boys would ask about him, but our son together was too young to know what was going on. After countless make ups and break ups, the cycle had to end because there was nothing left to piece back together.

I had given him more chances than I should have and the emotional pain was troublesome. Going back and forth with the same person was not changing the inevitable—my broken heart. Letting go was not easy, but I had to move on from that unfortunately flawed relationship. I did not want to jump right into dating, but I started to really like this guy that I had known for a while. He used to throw little hints to show me he was interested in me, but I was unavailable... until I wasn't anymore. I was not over my ex, but I wanted to be and hoped the new guy could help; I was hoping I wasn't rushing things.

We started to date and were spending a lot of time together that I was enjoying, might I add. He told me he was falling in love with me, but honestly, I still loved my ex and could not fully give my heart to him. He was a gentleman, a real honest and caring man who just wanted to love me and I was afraid to let him. He adored me and would do anything to make me happy, but yet, I could not stop thinking about my ex... it was complicated. When I saw him, his smile greeted me before his hug did and I would melt in the comfort of his strong arms.

Why do we always let those types of men get away only to run back to undeserving, broken little boys who cannot tell their front from their back?

My ex was not giving up. He kept pulling on my heartstrings, telling me how much he loved and missed me; how sorry he was; how he would never hurt me again. I knew they were all lies, but it was not long until I started to believe him again. I was a fool. I tried to avoid him and not listen to his empty promises, but it failed. And just like that... It happened. I started to let him come back over and spend quality time with me while I was still seeing the other guy. He was nothing like my ex, but everything I wanted in a man. However, the ex had pieces of me I had never given to anyone. I had an amazing connection with the new guy and I was not ready to end it, but I knew somehow I had to politely break it off with him.

I allowed my ex to talk me into looking for an apartment for us to move into because the lease was almost over and he wanted a fresh start. I knew in my gut the other guy deserved me, but the ex had my heart and we shared a child. God knows I did not want to have a third absent father from another child of mine's life. Plus, he loved my other two son's as his own and promised we would be a family... I wanted that so badly.

The guy I was seeing deserved to know I was getting back with my ex and we were moving in together. On top of that, I had to tell my mom she and my sisters had to find a place to go because they could not move into our new apartment. The weight was heavy, but I did what I thought was best for my children and I. The boys did not know the new guy, but they knew my ex who suddenly became my boyfriend again and he was the person I chose to be in our lives. My intentions were good. The pressure of making this decision was heavy and probably going to be one I regretted, but I was willing to take the risk. He really did love me and hopefully the break-up helped him realize he needed to be devoted to his family.

The day came and with sadness in my heart and tears in my eyes the heartbreaking words came out of my mouth: "My ex-boyfriend and I are getting back together, I'm sorry."

The stunned look on his face said it all. I knew I shouldn't have dated him after a painful breakup. He was so hurt and could not understand why I would go back to someone who hurt me, but he wanted me to be happy. As he wrapped his arms around me, I felt his tears on my shoulder and the tightness of his squeeze not wanting to let me go. When he finally walked away, I felt a piece of me go with him; I really liked him. He was good for me and I'll be honest, deep down inside I developed a love for him that I did not want to part from.

I never wanted to cause him any pain and he deserved better than me, I just wished I could have loved him fully. We worked at the same hospital, so I had to see him daily. Every time he saw me, he would say, "I love you and when he messes up, I'll be right here."

He never stopped being kind to me and he continued to greet me with that big smile and comforting hug. His cologne seemed to be embedded in me; I'd smell him for hours before it would fade away. I truly missed him and the time we spent together, but I had to let it go. However, it did not stop me from thinking about him.

The Unexpected Woes

It was time to move into our new apartment in less than two weeks. I was packing boxes while hoping I made the right choice being back with my ex-boyfriend.

My mother and sisters were moving in with one of my mom's good girlfriends. I was worried because she would be in the center of the city with easier access to drugs. I prayed she would do well, but I could no longer be responsible for her choices.

One day, out of nowhere, this sharp pain in my stomach emerged. I felt like I was going to die. I laid down hoping it would go away, but it did not. I was praying to God to at least ease the pain, because none of the pain medication I took worked. I called my boyfriend crying, telling him about the pain, and he tried to comfort me until I fell asleep. Soon after, the same pain awakened me. I rocked back and forth, asking God, "If it's my time, take me."

I could not take it any longer. It was worse than child labor pains. *What was wrong with me?* My mother, worried and scared, said, "I'm calling the ambulance."

When they arrived, I could barely stand up straight, let alone walk. The ride to the hospital lying flat on a stretcher felt like eternity. I was crying like a baby, holding my mother's hand with so many questions running through my mind about what was wrong. Once we arrived, the wait wasn't long before getting me set up for X-rays; I think they had an idea of what was wrong based on my symptoms. When my results came back the doctor told me that I had gallstones... I was relieved I was not dying.

Okay, what does that mean? The doctor explained why my pain was so excruciating; I had a blockage. There was a big stone on my gallbladder that was blocking the smaller stones that would have passed. The smaller stones that were not able to get through are what caused the most pain, but the gallbladder had to be removed. Before the removal of my gallbladder, I had to have a procedure to suck all of the small stones out, and then the next day the gallbladder would be removed. It was a lot to take in, but I wanted whatever needed to be done. It was a Sunday night, and my procedure could not get scheduled until Thursday, then the gallbladder surgery for Friday. I had to be admitted to the hospital. *Who would take care of my three sons*—1, 3, and 5 years of age?

Also, we're scheduled to move, *who's going to do all of that?* My mind was spinning with questions as I was the person always in control of everything, but then I had to trust others to take care of my responsibilities.

Mostly everything was packed previously before I was taken to the hospital, thank God. My mother and boyfriend told me not to worry; of course, I did. Relaxing was something a rarely did, but I had no choice that time. My main concern was for my children, although I knew between the two of them (mother and boyfriend), the kids would be fine. To top it all off, I wondered about my boyfriend's ability to stay faithful, we had just gotten back together. Although, that should have been the least of my worries the thoughts were there.

Once my mother left the hospital that night, she never came back to see me again nor did I hear from her. I was calling her, but she was not home, it did not make sense why she didn't check on me knowing I would be having surgery. I questioned my boyfriend about her whereabout and he told me she and my sisters moved from the old apartment, leaving him with the kids. He had to get help from his mom to watch the kids and move our things into the new apartment. My feelings were hurt, but regardless, all I wanted was for my mother and sister's to be okay and adjust to where they were.

After being released from the hospital, I still worried about the well-being of my mother. I had not heard from her, and it truly bothered me. Once I settled in at home, although I was in so much pain and discomfort, I had to call my mom's friend to see how she was doing. When I called asking if she was there, which she was, I could not wait to ask her why she never came back to see me or at least call. When she came to the phone, it sounded as if something was wrong, and our conversation felt distant. Instead of me asking her why she did not come back to the hospital, I gently said, "I thought you were coming back to see me, and you didn't, are you okay?"

She had no real explanation, and I was so disappointed at her lack of concern for me. Actually, I felt sad and hurt!

Before hanging up, my mom's friend wanted to speak to me privately. She told me that my mom was using drugs every day and needed help. Honestly, I could not deal with that, and I was tired of her choosing the drugs over her children, it was so damaging. "If my mom wanted help, she is going to have to do it herself, I cannot do it for her," I said.

I had to pray for her and turn it over to God. I was there for her as much as I could, but there was nothing I could do for her at the time; I needed to physically heal myself. I wasn't trying to be mean, I wanted to help her, I just wasn't sure if I could. My main concern was getting better, and I don't think she understood what she was doing to all of her children.

The Battles of a Fresh Start

At this point, it was several weeks since we moved into our new apartment and I loved it, however, I was still concerned about my mom. I wanted to understand her addiction, but it was hard to deal with. Each day I felt better and better after the surgery and wished my mom was with me. It seemed I should have been doing more to get her some help or perhaps admitted into a rehabilitation center, but I could not force her. The life decisions she had made were hers and hers alone for whatever reason. After all those years of her using drugs on and off, I knew there was nothing I could do to actually stop her from running back to it.

Finally, my life had to come first and my boyfriend was a part of that, my mom chose her life… and it was time for me to choose mine.

I was so happy and falling completely in love with my boyfriend again, especially because of how he stepped up while I was in the hospital and managed to come see me every day and took care of the kids. I really was seeing a new man and I was well pleased—no drugs and no cheating. I believe we were in our apartment a month before the question was popped with a ring and on one knee, He said, "Will you marry me?" "Yes, yes, and yes!" I screamed.

I was trusting love again and was fully living in that moment of happiness.

I loved that man, and I could not wait to be his wife and spend the rest of my life with him. Plus, it was the Godly and right thing to do this time, instead of living like we were married.

Marrying him would be easy, especially with the changes he was making, and I hoped it was not temporary. We did not want to waste any time, so we gave ourselves three months to plan our wedding. We told our families. Some were happy and others not so much. They said things like, "What's the rush?" and "Why so soon, y'all just got back together?"

While the others said, "I'm so happy for you two." and "Congrats, looking forward to the big day!"

I called my dad and his wife to tell them and they were super happy, offering to pay for my wedding dress. I did not see much of my dad, but I loved him and wanted him to be a part of my special day to walk me down the aisle because that's what dads do. I waited to tell my mother last because for some reason she stopped liking him and it seemed like she did not like me that much either at times. When I finally told her, her response was so cold, and she was not happy at all, telling me not to ask her for anything and she did not want to be a part of it. Needless to say, I was heartbroken and questioned why she wouldn't be proud of me. I just figured I would give her some time to change her mind. I wished her reaction was different, in fact I wanted her to embrace the idea that her oldest daughter was getting married.

It was time for me to go back to work after being off for six weeks for the surgery. It was very likely that I would be running into the guy I dated at the hospital. After several days back at work, I had the nerve to talk with him about my proposal. I had to tell him I was getting married and so I called down to his department asking him to meet me at our spot. I do not know why I was so nervous and uncomfortable to break the news to him, so I just said it, "He asked me to marry him, I said 'yes,' and the wedding is in a few months." Disappointment in his eyes was followed by, "Congratulations, I wish you the best" then he slowly walked away, only looking back once.

Why was I standing there; did I want him to come back, sweep me in his arms, and run away with me? I did not know. Every day after that when I saw him at work it was not the same, he barely wanted to speak to me, but the wave was sufficient enough.

But what was my motivation for telling him, was I expecting him to change my mind? I had to tell him, and he needed to hear it from me, because of his feelings for me. With only a few months before the big day, I had no choice but to forgot about what we shared, but I thought of him often. I was excited to be marrying the man I was in love with, and I did the right thing by having that face-to-face conversation with him. Nothing or no one else mattered, it was time to focus on planning my wedding; I only had a few months!

<u>Plans Derailed</u>

One day, I got a phone call—it's my youngest sister crying, begging me to come get her because she had not seen my mom in a couple of days. I was in the middle of planning a wedding and for the first time attempting to live my own life and be happy, but my sister needed my attention. I had to get her, and my fiancé did not mind. Once again, she was in the middle of our mother's troubled drug life and she didn't deserve that, none of us did. I wanted to explain my mother's addiction and habit to her, but I didn't know how. I knew my sister saw things because she was with her most of the time, I was not sure if she understood what our mother was really doing. She adored our mother and so did I, but at times she did not make it easy to. My mother and I had a bittersweet relationship, but we loved one another so much. Somehow the drugs distracted her from her children. She gave us all she had, but it was not enough; I always felt like I needed something deeper from her as a mother. I kept expecting her to be more than she was capable of being. Coming to grips with the fact that she did all she knew how to do was a hard truth I had to accept. For once, I wished life could be simple. This was supposed to be a happy and joyous time for me, but somehow, I always ended up on the back burner to take care everybody else.

Then, my mother called asking about my sister after coming back from another drug binge. This was so unusual for her; she was getting high nearly every day, something she had not done in the past. While we were talking, she started crying, saying she was tired and her friend that she was living with told her she had to leave her house. What was I supposed to do with this? We were living in another two-bedroom apartment and I was expected to house my mom and siblings—again?! I did not even know how to ask my fiancé if they could come stay with us until she figured out other living arrangements, but I had to. Where else would she go? After the way my mom had treated us, we still made sure she was good and he agreed to let her and my other sister stay with us, since my youngest was already there. *Was I making another mistake*? Of course, I was, but I did it anyway.

Once I got them to the apartment, I could not talk to my mother. I waited until the next day. She looked awful; she had lost so much weight I could barely stand to see her like that. What happened to my mother? Why was she abusing herself with drugs? It was something I could not wrap my head around. The next morning, we talked and all she could do was cry and apologize for how she had treated me and for not coming back to the hospital. She wanted me to help her with the addiction; she did not want to do drugs anymore. But I was not convinced... it was just an emotional plea. I knew while she was with me there would be a chance of her staying away from drugs temporarily because we didn't live close to the city.

She finally said she wanted to be a part of the wedding, asking how she could help. But then right after, she became very emotional. She was calling herself ugly and said how skinny she was. I cried , hugged her, and told her she was beautiful... I forgave her.

She was deeply wounded and struggling, and drugs were her pain medicine for some reason. I wanted to strip her permanently of the drugs, but I was powerless and helpless in that area; she needed to do it for herself.

I could not stay mad at her I loved my mother dearly. Plus, she agreed to be a part of the wedding, which was delightful to hear, but honestly all I wanted was for her to be there and that was more than enough for me. My mother needed me, and I needed and wanted whatever she had left to give... which I knew was very little. I had always been there for her, making sure she was secure, especially in a crisis. It really felt good to finally be able to share my wedding and excitement with her and see her smile. She worried about what she would wear. I did not want her to worry about anything. I was going to make sure she would look beautiful.

One day, while I was working, I received a phone call from my mother crying, and I could hardly make out her words. In a panic, I told my supervisor I needed to leave because my mother was in trouble. Once I arrived at home, she was lying in bed in so much pain, saying her head was hurting so badly she could not raise it up from the pillow. We were both crying because we did not know what was wrong. I called the ambulance and frantically waited by my mother's side. So many thoughts were running through my mind. I did not want to lose her, but I could not help but think the worst while hoping for the best. The ambulance finally arrived; what took less than 15 minutes seemed like a lifetime. I followed behind the ambulance, praying that mom would be alright. My mother was a type 1 diabetic, but Lord knows I did not think that was the culprit until the doctor said, "Your mother's blood sugar was over 700 and had she not come in today, she would have died."

I believe the drugs and not taking her insulin before coming to live with me almost costed her her life. She had to be admitted to the hospital until her blood sugars and pressure were regulated. I felt relieved knowing my mother was going to live and not die. I hated the lifestyle she was living, but she was the only person who could change the outcome.

After about a week in the hospital, she was discharged. I was doing my best as a mother of three, fiancé, daughter and sister, on top of going to work. With all the madness that was going on around me I still had to keep it together, but it was starting to take a toll on me. I had a wedding to plan and had to get back to what was important to me. Thank God, my fiancé's mother had a lot of the details arranged along with the wedding coordinator. I do not know how I would have managed without them; they made it less stressful.

I was so happy as the days were getting closer, but then a very close friend of mine, who later became friends with my fiancé, wanted to have a talk with me. When a person asks if they can meet with you just to talk, is that ever all it is?

I was not expecting to hear, "Are you sure you are ready to get married?"

I wanted to know why he would ask me this, what did he know that he was not telling me—was he protecting me or indirectly warning me? After my mind went racing, he said, "I just wanted to make sure you were ready, I am happy for y'all."

Was that totally true? Hugging me, he asked me to keep our conversation between us, which felt strange. Why did he do this to me a few weeks before my big day, causing so much doubt and confusion in my mind? It only grew, and I became suspicious. I focused so much on that conversation that it was starting to get the best of me. When my fiancé was not present in the home, I wondered whether he was where he said he was or with whom he said he was with. *This cannot be happening; what does my friend know?*

I had to shake those thoughts. I was about to marry the man I was ready to spend the rest of my life with. He changed, right? We got baptized together!…

Should I tell him what our friend said? Should I start snooping through his things? No, just trust him, is what I told myself.

I had to be excited for my bridal shower, last day dress fitting, and wedding rehearsal. So, I carried on with the anticipation of meeting him at the altar.

19 and pregnant with baby boy number 3.

Me and my 3 sons.

My youngest son.

133

THE UNVEILING

CHAPTER 10

ALL THINGS NEW

(Married Life)

I am ready to marry my man on this beautiful sunny day, 08-08-1993 at 3 p.m.

I woke up on top of the world, smiling ear to ear. My maid of honor, bridesmaids, and the whole wedding party were thrilled and filled with joy, just as I was. The closer it got to the time the more nervous I became. I wanted everything to be perfect—I had been waiting for that moment for a while. I had so many worries: *Was the limousine going to be on time? Will the guests arrive on time? Is every flower in its place? Will I make it down the aisle with my daddy without crying?*

And one big question lingered way in the back of my mind: Am I making the right decision? I tried to assure myself.

Of course, I am; we love each other. Our life will be imperfectly perfect.

Finally, it was time to load up in the limousine. I could not believe I was about to "tie the knot." It was only a 15-minute drive to the church, but it seemed like forever! We waited in front of the church watching the last few guests arrive. My heart was beating fast. Then, it was time to exit the limo. The wedding party all went before me, then it was my time.

"All guests please stand, as the bride is about to enter."

I walked down the aisle to stand in front of my man as our family and friends witnessed our union before God and saying our vows to one another. We looked one another in the eyes and the tears fell down his face, which was my proof that this man really loves me.

"Who gives this woman to be married to this man?" said the pastor.

"I do," my father said, and just like that he handed me over to my husband and we became one. The wedding day was beautiful, the reception was amazing, our family and friends were blissful, and our weekend getaway was abundantly full of love and togetherness.

The Marriage

The wedding day and your actual marriage are not the same, contrary to what some believe. After getting married, it was time to begin our lives as husband and wife, but something was hanging over our heads. My mother and sisters were still living with us, and I was uncertain how it was going to work. We agreed to let them stay for a little while longer, but only if my mother was actively looking for a place to move.

Not long into our marriage, I noticed my mother starting to treat my husband like she hated him. He would walk in from work, and she would not speak to him. He pulled me aside about it and I had to confront her, telling her she needed to at least say hello. She was not happy about it and felt like I was forcing her to speak. *Are you serious, it is not forcing it's called being polite!*

For the life of me I could not understand where this friction or tension was coming from. It disturbed me, but as usual, I ignored my feelings and hoped things would get better.

136

About six weeks into our marriage, my husband lost his job. I tried to be a supportive wife. But then I started to notice other things—he was gone away from the home more than he should have been, being a new husband and all. I just assumed he did not want to be around my family, which I understood, so I did not think too much about it. Doing so did not help him win my mother's approval of our marriage; it only added more fuel to the fire. She was sure to let me know he did not deserve me. Home was becoming unpleasant and the tension was so thick that you could cut it with a knife. The honeymoon was over before it even started; I guess we left it at our weekend getaway.

My husband would come home and before coming to bed would always shower, which was not at all uncommon, but because of our past history I made it out to be more than it was. *I have to get those thoughts out of my head, he was not cheating or hiding something he just would not do that to me again.*

One day, he walked out into the common area where my mother, sisters, and I were sitting with a towel wrapped around his waist. That seemed odd and disrespectful to me. When he walked back into our bedroom, I went behind him expressing my thoughts and asking him to never do that in front of my family again. He did not see it as a big deal but apologized and agreed not to do it again. I was not feeling like a happy bride, and the conversation I had with my friend started to surface in my mind again. *What was happening here? We were still newly married, and it was too soon for it to be falling apart.* In situations like this, communication was key, and I wanted to save my marriage. But I felt trouble heading our way.

One evening, my husband came home and once again he spoke to my mother and she said nothing back. I mean was I missing something, why all of a sudden did she despise him? Why was she doing this? I had to get to the bottom of it. After she blatantly did not speak, he said to her, "You cannot stay in my house and not speak."

I tried to step in to be the peacemaker because I knew she was going to fly off the handle and she did!

All hell broke loose after that. My mother did not take too kindly to him saying anything to her and I could not control the argument. I was not expecting him to say, "You need to get out of my house."

My mother continued to argue back with him, not making it easy for me to control the situation. *Now, what am I going to do? Do I put my husband's feelings on the backseat making my mother my priority?*

I had to honor my husband and he was not going to change his mind about her leaving, nor was she going to change her mind and stay. It was a sad situation, my mother had to be triggered by something. There was no moving this mother and son-in-law forward.

She made a phone call to a relative asking if they could come there to live and they agreed. The next day, I moved them in with a family member. My mother made no attempt to reconcile, she was ready to leave; there was an enormous amount of friction between them two. Surely, I did not want it to end like that, but my mother made it impossible for me to support her on this. I felt a sharp pain in my heart after she left. I was devastated about what took place, wishing I could have fixed it. I loved them both! There was nothing I could say that was going to change how she felt about him, especially not after that argument. I hated my children and sisters had to witness it all, especially my youngest, she'd been through enough.

Trust No One

My husband had introduced me to one of his female friends who became a good friend to me. After what happened between my mother and husband, I called to talk to her about the situation. The argument had hit me differently, and I didn't know what to do about it. She was a good listener that gave sound advice, and I needed to discuss my concerns. She helped me to see that clearly neither of them wanted to change and my husband was beyond frustrated with my mother. She advised me not to let it negatively affect my marriage, but I was still hurting over it. One quiet evening, I replayed the argument between my mother and husband in my head, and as clear as day I remembered my mother saying, "He is not who you think he is, you will find out he is not shit."

What did she mean? Did she know something I did not? Why were people constantly raising doubt in my mind? I tried to forget about it, but I had to ask my husband what my mother meant. He said, "I have no idea, you know your mother do not like me."

Did that answer make sense or was I just a pure blind fool? I do not know. But this surely was not the marriage I intended to have. It was like I was trying to regain the trust of my husband again, was there a need for that?

I just went on with life trying to be a loving wife while my husband was out looking for another job. His female friend was always such a big help to us because we only had one car, so she would take him around to fill out applications and I appreciated that. I confided in her a lot; she was an older woman and always seemed to have the right answer at the right time.

I tried to have some type of normalcy in my life, but something always shifted my plans. My job was changing their hours and it affected me because they went by seniority. I waited patiently for them to finally tell me that I would be working night shift—11 p.m. to 7 a.m. My first thought was, *I cannot work that shift with three small children*, but then reality kicked in that I was the only one with income.

I only had a couple of days to prepare for my new shift and my husband seemed to take the news well, so that made the load a little lighter. He stayed home with the children while I worked nights, what else was he going to do. They were so young, almost 2, 4, and 5 years of age. Those nights were kicking my butt and I was extremely exhausted, barely getting any sleep. When I came home in the mornings, I had to take my oldest to school, which he was only there for half of the day. On the days my husband had the car, he would pick him up from school, which allowed me more time to rest through the morning.

My husband was really starting to change; he was gone all of the time and I started to see some of the same behaviors from when he used to do drugs. *Was he doing drugs again? If so, how did I miss that, or was I just too tired to notice?*

Our marriage took a turn, I began to feel the mistrust and it was causing some issues. I did not want to jump to conclusions, but something was not right, and I was going back and forth in my mind trying to figure it out.

One Saturday evening, one of his good friends came over to our house. I opened the door to tell him my husband was not home, but he asked to come in. I saw nothing wrong with that because they had been childhood friends and I knew him too; he was no stranger. We were talking about a bunch of nothing and all of a sudden, he said, "Do not trust him because he is cheating on you."

What?

He told me not to tell my husband, but how do I keep this secret? I asked him questions about who the person was, and he said it was with people I knew who were very close to me. I asked, "Who? Please tell me."
But he would not. He said, "You will soon find out."

Now what type of friend was he, yet I did needed to hear it, but was it true?

How does everyone know about my husband, except for me? Then he proceeded to tell me how pretty I was and how he would be a better a man for me. *Okay, it's time for you to go.*

I wanted to avoid having this conversation with my husband, however he needed to know.

I was drowning with emotions and my head was spinning from everything his friend told me. When my husband came home, I confronted him at the door and of course he said, "He is lying."

I wanted to believe him and so I said you are probably right because he tried to come on to me. My husband then used that information by saying, "He told you that because he was trying to get with you! I'm going to kick his ass for disrespecting you and me."

Yeah, it made sense not to trust the friend! He could not believe that his friend flirted with me and lied about him cheating on me. I believed my husband. He had a way of convincing me that the words coming out of his mouth was the truth.

One morning, getting off from work, I rushed home to get my son ready for school. I was not prepared for what happened next. While I was driving him to school he said, "Mommy, I have to tell you something, but you have to promise me you will not say nothing."

"What is it?"

"You have to promise."

"Okay, I promise."

"Last night, I saw a woman in the house."

"Wait, what? Are you sure?"

"Yes, someone knocked on the door and then he let her in. He thought we were sleep but I was still up. I saw her walk by and go in your room and he shut the door behind them."

"You are not making this up, are you?"

"No, Mommy. She went in the kitchen and warmed up food in the microwave. She had a scarf on her head."

I was shaking. I could not control myself. My baby was not lying; no one was lying. *Who did I marry?*

I told my son, "Mommy is sorry, but I have to break my promise."

I told him not to worry, he was not in trouble. After I dropped him off, I sped to get back in that house to storm in like lightning.

"Who the hell did you have in my house last night and do not lie?!" I asked.
Every lie that he could tell… he told. But I assured him that my 5-year-old son would not know to make up a detailed story like the one he told me. He continued to lie, and I wanted to believe him so badly, but I knew he was lying.

Later, he picked up my son from school. When he came in, he said, "Mommy, I lied to you, there was nobody here last night."

He had convinced my baby that what he saw was not real. After my husband left, my son told me that he made him say it was not true. There really was a woman in the house. He said, "I saw her."

My marriage was falling apart—it was crumbling. All of the warnings were there, and I did not take heed to any of them. I wanted to believe he had changed and was being honest. I could no longer trust him. I shared my feelings with his female friend, telling her exactly what he did to me, and she wanted me to be sure my son was telling the truth and had me challenge the credibility of the other people too. How did I go from believing my baby to second-guessing him and thinking *maybe he thought he saw a woman?*

I wanted my marriage to work—it was not a year in, and it had been one thing after another. I decided I was going to try to believe in my husband and commit to our vows for better or worse.

Finally, he found a job. We were so excited, but something was not right—I could not turn my women's intuition off. Why would my son lie about seeing a woman in the house? The truth of the matter was, my son told me exactly what he saw that night. My husband did not appreciate what he had at home, and he was willing to risk losing everything. Although, I was happy he found another job it was not enough, our marriage had hit a brick wall. I was becoming unhappy and I was holding on by a thread to save what was left of my already broken marriage. Maybe my mother was right when she said he was not shit, I was finding that to be truer.

I asked him again to tell me about that night and he continued to say, "I am not cheating. You are my wife and I love you."

Was I just a fool, did I really want to be married that bad or was I crazy in love, what was it? I was tired of trying to keep up with his lies, it was driving me away, but not far enough.

Our rental lease was about to end, and we needed to decide our next move. I wanted to be loved by this man so badly that I became blind to the truth that was staring me in the face. Every time my husband left the home, I worried about what he was doing; it was draining and exhausting, but I still tried to be the good wife. He lied compulsively and it was not helping our marriage... we needed counseling.

One night, he came in the house furious with me. We got into a huge argument, and he accused me of telling his female friend our business. I saw nothing wrong with talking to her, but she was not honest about what I shared with her. I trusted her; how could she betray me like that? Nothing was adding up. I started to wonder about her, which I had no reason to before. I called and cursed her out, telling her she was no longer allowed in my home and I wanted nothing else to do with her and to stay away from my family and husband. I told him I did not want her around anymore and he grudgingly agreed as he was trying to take her side and switch the story around.

I was not sure if I wanted to be married any longer, he had become a stranger. Could our marriage be salvaged?

I didn't want to give up too soon, but the happy marriage was failing, and I didn't know how to save it.

Things escalated and got completely out of control. As challenging as my marriage was, we needed to make it work because our lease was soon up and we wanted to move into something more spacious. I told myself *no marriage is perfect and maybe I was misinterpreting things.*

I hoped that when we moved that we could effectively work through our issues and feelings and pay more attention to strengthening our marriage. I had never seen an example of a healthy marriage or relationship before; I just wanted my family to stay together.

My husband had a friend who was renting out his three-bedroom townhouse and said he would rent it to us as long as we had the security deposit and first month's rent. We went to look at the house together and fell in love with it. I was hoping it could be a fresh start for our marriage.

The only thing I did not like was the location. It was in Baltimore City, but a really nice area. Not too bad, I could adapt. So, we agreed that we would accept the offer and rent the townhouse.

144

All Hell Broke Loose

After moving into our new place, I felt we were getting close and starting to mend the trust that had been broken in our marriage. But after a few weeks, I began to notice some changed patterns of behavior again. My husband had to be to work at 6 a.m., I knew he was getting a ride, and I assumed it was from a coworker. One morning, my gut was telling me to look out the window—the car he got into was the female friend we agreed could no longer be a part of our lives.

I was devastated; how could he double-cross me like that? Later that evening when he returned home, I questioned him about who was picking him up in the morning. He looked me dead in my face and said, "My buddy from work."

The rage that came out of me was like a roaring lion ready to attack. Why did I expect so much from this man? Everyone tried to warn me about him, including my baby boy. Even after telling him I saw the car he got into, he still made every attempt to lie. "Why would she be coming all the way on the other side of town to pick you up? Are you sleeping with her?" I asked.

Why did I ask him questions when I knew he would just lie? My heart was breaking into tiny little pieces and I could not catch my breath. I had been married to a liar and cheater, and there was nothing he could do to get me to ever trust him again, it was officially damaged. No apology, time, communication, or reasoning… bottom line, I was done.

I wanted him out of the house—I couldn't stand looking at him any longer. I had three little people I was responsible for and I had allowed them around this dysfunction for far too long. He refused to leave the home, and every day that he stayed I grew more resentful of him and our marriage. I could not prove he was sleeping with his friend, but I knew he was. *The woman in my house that night, was it her?*

She was the woman my 5-year-old son was talking about. Our marriage had run its course and this time there was no getting back together, it had to end!

I had driven myself crazy in the marriage and I knew I should have walked away long before then, but I stayed. After you have stayed in a marriage by yourself, giving everything to make it work and then you burn out, there is no more fight left. My marriage was not easy, he lost respect for our vows while I was still holding on. It was a losing battle. I was fighting to be loved, honored, stay sane and to keep my family together and I did not win. I tried to excuse all of his bad behaviors by placing the blame on his addiction and being too young to handle a family of five. In doing so, I was emotionally and physically exhausted in my marriage almost to the point of denying reality, facts, and truth.

On New Year's Eve, we got into an argument and I knew he had to leave after that. We had emotionally abandoned each other and said things we could not take back. I felt very little-to-no connection between us and I did not want to explode again around the children, but his refusal to leave only caused more rage.

On New Year's Day, 1995, after sleeping on it, my mind did not change, which took courage on my part. He thought he was going to have a rest day. Wrong! I said, "Here are some trash bags—pack your stuff and go."

He refused to leave until I got crazy again. He was yelling that it was his house too. "I think not, what bills have you paid?" I asked. "Do not make me throw your clothes out of the window!"

The time to break free was then and there, I'm not sure why he did not know that. Although, it was painful for him to leave, staying would have been worst, he finally packed his clothes and left. After only one and a half years of marriage, it was over!

CHAPTER 11

WHAT IS DONE IN THE DARK

(It Came to the Light)

Things done in the dark hours of night, behind closed doors, or in the heat of the moment looked a lot different in the morning, out in the open, and with a clear head.
—Penelope Douglas

My marriage was over, and I had become angry and regretful about my decision to end it. He was not the husband I imagined I would be married to—or was this who he was all along? Maybe I assumed marriage would change him, but it only made him, and us, worse. I did not go into this marriage expecting things to be perfect. Why make vows before family, friends, and God if there was no intent to honor them? Was I to blame for ignoring the dreadful truth, or was I too scared to live life without him? Whatever it was I could not keep staying in a marriage like a caged bird flying in circles and ending up in the same place.

I needed to vent, so I reached out to my friend who asked me before getting married was I sure. He already knew my husband and I had separated; there was no need to rehearse that. He allowed me to verbalize all of my feelings, emotions, rage and regret; he just listened. Once, I said, "I think I am going to reconcile my marriage. This is crazy talk, no way."

I was not expecting him to say, "No, you did the right thing."

Why would he say that? What does he know? Did I really want to hear the truth—was I ready for that? I asked, "What do you mean I did the right thing?"

<u>The Betrayal</u>

What came out of his mouth did more than blow me away; it shattered my soul leaving me flabbergasted and wondering if I believed what he was saying. There are some truths that can turn your life upside down leaving your jaw on the floor. When he told me my husband was cheating on me during our engagement and our marriage with multiple women, I was left feeling paralyzed. He had details, names, times, and locations of where he would cheat and some of the women he slept with. I was as shocked as a groom waiting for his bride who never shows up, never saw that happening. It left me totally stunned, blindsided, and stupefied I honestly wanted to vomit. I knew I was not dreaming; I was fully awake, but somehow I went numb and I didn't want to feel or hear anymore words that were coming out of his mouth.

I asked, "Why are you telling me all of this now? How could you keep this from me?"

He tried to tell me that he wanted me to know the truth before the wedding. He did not want to hurt me and hoped my husband would change and commit to our marriage. As if what he already told me was not gut-wrenching enough, the last blow was the woman who befriended me had been sleeping and doing drugs with my husband all along. I thought to myself, *I figured that*, although I was still crushed. My heart stopped beating and I needed to catch my breath as the tears rolled down my face. I was in disbelief; *this could not be real.*

"How does a person who said they loved you do all of this?" I

148

asked.

"He wanted to break me down and he did."

I was sick about what I was told. I replayed every scenario in my head, every lie and excuse, all the manipulation and deception, and every telltale sign. *How could I be so stupid and foolish?* I screamed to the top of my lungs, "How could you do this to me?"

Although, our marriage was over the betrayal left me floored and emotionally traumatized. None of it felt good and I needed to hear the truth from my husband. I was mindful that he struggled with telling the truth, but I hoped he would at the least come clean. The call to him was dreadful, I could not handle anymore lies, but I wanted to give him the opportunity to be honest with me. He made every attempt to deny it, making me more furious and anger started bubbling up. "Just tell the damn truth!" I begged him to tell me.

I just needed to hear him say it. And finally, in a sobering and dreadful tone, he admitted it. An intense feeling took control of my mind. I saw red and smelled blood. I felt like I became unhinged in my thoughts. Admittedly, I wanted everyone dead—I hated all of them. I did not feel human.

I hung up and started crying uncontrollably. This whole thing left a nasty taste in my mouth and I was in unbearable agony. Obviously, he was out of the house, but the residue of the turmoil was lingering all around my heart. I did not want to torment myself by asking the same questions over and over again. But I was still human and in between my emotions and the shock of it all.

I woke up the next morning hoping everything that I had heard was not true... but it was. After gathering my thoughts, I decided to call up an old friend. I wanted him to hurt my husband and he was ready to do it. I knew it was not the right thing to do, but I wanted him to be trampled by a bull. There's nothing quite like a woman scorned. But how would I explain to my son that his father was dead or badly hurt? However, that was exactly what I wanted to happen. I was so angry and full of tremendous resentment. But I ended up calling it off, feeling sick to my stomach that I had those thoughts, but I wanted him to suffer in the worst way possible.

Changing Lanes

It was about two months after the separation and I was still healing. As the days went on, I did experience some emotional ups and downs, especially when there was contact with my husband concerning the children. I had never been married before; therefore, I was in uncharted territory trying to figure out how to live my life as a married, yet single, woman. It was hard for me because I still had to be a mom, work, and take care of responsibilities that did not disappear because my marriage did.

My bills were insurmountable; I was not bringing in enough money to compensate my expenses and my husband was not helping me with anything. I was drowning in bills and my rent was behind and catching up would only put me behind again. How was I going to get myself out of this financial rut? It was too much to think about, but it could not be ignored!

I explained the situation to my landlord; he was sympathetic about my separation and made every attempt to help me by not charging late fees or taking me to court. I continued to fall behind, and I did not see how I could bounce back. Every wall around me was closing in and the spaces seemed to get smaller and tighter; I was suffocating. I did not want to move from my house, but I could not see another way. My children deserved stability and security, not this. I felt guilty as a mother with no solutions to the mountain of responsibilities I was left to carry alone. These unknown circumstances were stressing me out because I had nowhere else to go being a family of four. Sure, I had family and a few friends who would not see us on the street, but we needed our own space. However, I kept reminding myself that *we would get through this difficult time and move forward somehow.*

One morning on my way to work while riding the subway, I saw this guy—a cute one, might I add. I had seen him a couple times before, but this particular day we locked eyes but did not say a word until it was nearly time to get off at our stop. He walked over to me asking for my name and if he could call me. I smiled nervously and asked for his number. He laughed and said, "You're not going to call me."

As he gave me his number I thought, *Throw it away and do not waste your time.* But he was handsome with a really nice body; I wanted to see what he had to offer. Perhaps I was looking for a rebound to fix what was shattered on the inside, *my heart.*

I was spiritually, mentally, physically, emotionally, and financially broken, that man does not need me in his life. Every area of my life was in pieces and I was far from needing another man. I could not even think about committing myself to another person. *I was jumping the gun, it was too soon to be thinking like this.* I was grieving the loss of my marriage and it was twisted in knots that could not be easily untangled. Day by day I was starting to move on and the sadness was lifting little by little, nonetheless I was feeling depressed. But I wondered if I had room in my life for another person with everything I was dealing with. Did I need someone interrupting my or our lives?

As I pondered on whether to make that call, deep down inside I wanted to know if he could be different. *What the hell?* I called anyway. Why was I so nervous as the phone rang? I asked for him and he was not available. My mind raced with doubt, I wished I had never called. Why did I reach out to him?

Soon thereafter, he called me back. I was speechless, but happy to hear his voice, I did not know what to say. I was vulnerable and trying to get back to a regular routine, but something new was refreshing at the time. He had just broken up with his girlfriend— literally like that same day. Maybe I should have hung up and never talked to him again. But he was charming and saying all of the right things, at least it was what I wanted to hear, although he sounded just as nervous as I did. I told him I had just separated from my husband and was still getting over the pain. I did not want to spend too much time talking about the breakup, but more time knowing him. Were my emotions driving the conversation? I could not make sense of anything that was happening, going back and forth from confusion to pursuing. I did not want to seem like a damsel in distress looking for this man to sweep me off my feet, making it appear like I needed him. Okay, maybe it was time to end our conversation for the night—I was saying too much and acting desperate, not sure he picked up on that being as though he was not ready to hang up. He asked if we could talk more tomorrow.

I gave it a shot. We talked for a couple of days before he invited me over to his house. It was too soon for me to be seeing anybody, but I went anyway. I walked up to the door and he hugged me, I could have stayed right there in his arms all night. As I walked behind him to his bedroom, I thought to myself, *no sex just talk*. Why did he take his shirt off? I wanted to spend that night getting to know him, not sexing him. His skin was so soft and lips even softer. I was not sure if it was his body or my desperation that made me want him more. I shared pieces of my broken heart with him and how I was not in a position to be in a serious relationship. I honestly did not know how to tell him what I needed from a man when he asked because I did not know what that looked like for myself. All of the men in my life just wanted sex, so I gave it to him too. I was not sure what else about me was desirable that he'd want.

After our night together, he wanted to spend more and more time with me and get to know my sons. I was reluctant to bring him around my children; I was not sure if he was the one, but two months into our relationship he started coming around and spending time with the children. I was falling more in love... or was I trying hard to forget my husband? I wanted to put my husband out of my mind. It was the part of my life I wished never existed, but it did and I could not erase him.

What I could not forget was that I was falling behind in my rent with no way to catch up. My temporary assignment at work had ended and I was jobless. *Do I tell the guy I am seeing I need financial help or risk getting evicted? Will the landlord keep being patient and understanding?* My husband was not helping me with anything. I ended up telling the new guy, and to my surprise he said he and his ex were about to move into an apartment before they broke up. *Where was he going with this?* He said, "I'm still moving, and you and your children can just move in with me."

I did not know what to do. I barely knew this man, but what other options did I have? My mother thought it was a bad idea, but I definitely was not considering how she felt at the time, I had to only think about my children and I. As much as I strongly disliked my husband, it was the right thing to do to tell him that the kids and I were moving in with my new man. He was not happy at all. He had some nerve to voice his opinion that I did not ask for, even though he was living with that woman who befriended me.

Moved Too Quickly

It was only three months later and I had a totally different life— it's like I blinked and was in another world. His family could not understand how he moved a woman and her three children into his apartment, hell I was wondering the same thing. They were troubled and questioned my motives, especially his mother. During the course of becoming a family, I had to make occasional changes and make the best of my new life with a man a hardly knew.

I wanted my mother and sister to come for a visit because I had not seen them in a couple of weeks. I had been so busy since the move, but I was missing the both of them so they came to stay a weekend with us. She liked the apartment but was not too fond of my boyfriend, she called him strange. But she respected how he was taking care of us. As long as I was happy, she was okay with it. Shortly after moving in together, I noticed some changes but I ignored them; I was good at looking but not seeing.

He began to show signs of jealousy and being controlling. As time went on his obsession became more apparent and visible, but I tried to call it cute, making myself believe it was not as bad as it seemed. *He was just being protective over me, there's nothing wrong with that.* This man was a hard worker and made good money, he took care of the bills and I took care of the home. I was tickled pink that he loved me so much that he wanted me all to himself. One day, he told me if something needed to be fixed in our apartment that he would take care of it. He did not want me calling the maintenance man for anything and he definitely did not want him in the apartment when he was not home, and we saw eye-to-eye on the matter. I didn't want to upset him. My man wanted to handle everything; I had a real one and this was all out of love.

I Became a Prisoner

It was a beautiful, sunny day outside, people were standing around talking and kids were playing—just a typical day. I was chatting with the maintenance man about a couple of things that needed to be fixed in the apartment, a very harmless conversation. I was not planning to let him come in the apartment; I was only sharing my concerns. My boyfriend had just gotten home from work and walked over to where we were standing. What happened next was unbelievable. "What's this? Didn't I tell you not to talk to him?" my boyfriend said. At first, I thought it was a joke, until I heard the seriousness in his tone followed by him punching the maintenance man in his face, which led to a fight between the two. I was so embarrassed over the scene he caused.

Someone called the police, but before they arrived, I was able to get my boyfriend into the house. The police did knock on our door asking what happened and informed us no charges would be filed because the other party said it was just a misunderstanding. Once they left, I did not know whether I should've packed my bags and ran or stayed and worked it out. I had never seen him act like that and I could not be certain I would not see it again. He apologized for his behavior, saying he saw me talking to the guy and lost his temper. *How many more times will you lose control?*

I jumped from one bad relationship to another one and I was frightened I had put my children and myself in harm's way. I had nowhere to go; sticking through this was all I could do. *Did I need to be on alert or was this an isolated incident?* While I was thinking it was cute, it was a serious problem. But he was so good to the kids and me; he loved us and provided a place for us to live. *It was just a bad day for him.* I continued in the relationship as if that day never happened, going along with it even though I didn't agree with what he had done. I noticed that every day he would come home from work and walk around the apartment and would ask, "Who has been in here?"

No matter how much I tried to reassure him that I was being faithful, he struggled to believe me.

What have I gotten myself into?

His jealousy only grew more intense. I was so nervous being in public with him anywhere; I never knew if I would do something to push his buttons and cause him to go into a rage. I was not allowed to look in the direction of another man, let alone speak to one. He accused me of doing things or acting in a way that drew attention to myself so other men would notice me. I only wanted him, but I found myself having to prove that all of the time. I wanted to leave, but I was between the security and stability he provided and the fear he embedded in me… so I stayed. Either way, I realized I rushed into this relationship too quickly!

The tension between him and the maintenance man was never resolved; it became so uncomfortable the rental office allowed us to break our lease. We were moving again in less than a year. It was ridiculous but for the best. We found a two-bedroom townhouse to move into and I was hoping things would change. I loved him and wanted to work on the relationship, especially after my failed marriage. I knew he was possessive, but he was never physical with me, so his jealousy did not seem that bad. I could not provide for my children and myself at the time, further making me feel emotionally and physically trapped. He so kindly took care of us and seemed to enjoy having a family. He had an estranged relationship with his son, but he treated my three sons like his own and I admired that. I made life for the children and I as happy and peaceful as I could, but it was not always easy. I often wondered when he would strike again, one minute things would be fine and the next something could trigger him. I tried to love him, but it was challenging and difficult at the same time. I was not ready to give up on him so I put my feelings aside, hoping he would improve.

Twists and Turns

I really missed my mom and baby sister as I often did when we were not together. I had not seen them for a few weeks at that point. I told my boyfriend I wanted to go see them and he made sure that I did. We drove to the house my mother was living at, and with excitement, I walked in. She was sitting around the dining room table with other relatives. I was smiling and thinking she would be happy to see me, but she was not—actually it was the opposite. I wanted to hug her, but the closer I got I realized why she did not even greet me with a smile after not seeing me for a while.

There it was… a needle stuck in her arm. I was tearful and disappointed. She held her head down and never acknowledged me, so I turned around and walked out without saying goodbye. She was getting high. And for the first time, I witnessed it. I know she felt embarrassed and ashamed. I was the last person she expected to see, especially in her state of being. I was angered at what I had seen, so much so I didn't even inquire about my sister, I just wanted out of there.

When I got to the car I started crying, quietly telling my boyfriend what happened so the kids could not hear me. After all of the years of my mother struggling with drugs, I never saw her physically inject the drugs into her arm. I wondered how she felt knowing what I had seen. My mother was losing the fight and I could not save her as she battled with drugs. I could not wait to get back home so my boyfriend could hold me in his arms; I just wanted to go to sleep and forget the image etched in my mind, but it would not go away.

I spent so much of my life trying to take care of my mother and it was not working, she was living her life and I had to live mine. One of my only concerns, as always, was the well-being of my sister. Although my mother was not deliberately choosing to use drugs, she had an addiction, and I could not allow it to keep mentally draining me. No matter how old I was, it was always a complicated situation I truly did not understand. At that point, it had been more than ten years since finding out my mother was an addict.

I have always worried about her dying and never coming back to us. This could very well have explained the fears I developed on top of the dependency to cling onto relationships. Brushing my feelings under the carpet, making excuses, and ignoring my mother' addiction had crept its way into my adulthood. At that point, I was with another man who I was staying with, despite his behaviors, so I would not feel the lack of love and attention I felt from my mother and father. After a few months living in the townhouse with this man and trying to make it work, I didn't know what else to do in this relationship that I had rushed full speed ahead into.

My brother and I were always close and one day him and our childhood friend came to visit while my boyfriend was still at work. I told him about what happened with our mother, which he hardly ever dealt with being in and out of trouble himself. He truly understood the weight I was carrying concerning our mother's addiction. He said, "Sis, let's just enjoy the afternoon."

And so we did. We were laughing, talking, and reminiscing on the old days. A couple hours later, I heard the keys in the door and my heart dropped. He walked in and looked directly at my childhood friend. He shook hands with my brother and he introduced him to our friend. While my boyfriend was shaking our friends hand, I saw that intense look on his face. He sat down in the chair across from him, asking random questions— one being how'd he know me, as if he were not introduced as a childhood friend. For a minute, I was nervous because my boyfriend did come on a little strong with the questions. But they were all getting along; to my surprise, everything seemed to be going well. Maybe I was tripping about the look. I needed to relax my tensed shoulders. *Everything will be fine, what could possibly go wrong?*

No sooner than I walked into another room I heard my boyfriend say, "Man, who are you? Are you messing with my girl?"

Oh no!

I walked back in the room to intervene. My brother and friend were trying to assure him I was like a sister, but he was not trying to hear that. Out of nowhere, he punched our friend in the face and a fight ensued. My brother and I tried to break it up. The kids were crying, and I was distraught, yet again. My brother told me to grab the kids and go. I rushed out of the house frantically knocking on my neighbor's door, and she let us in. I was so afraid of what was going to happen next.

I heard my boyfriend banging on the neighbor's door yelling, "You better let her out or I'm going to break this door down!"

She wanted to call the police, but I begged her not to. I told her I would just leave. When I came out, he was yelling in my face saying, "You going to bring somebody to my house you fucking?"

I did everything I could to defend myself, begging him to stop and go in the house. My brother had finally got our friend in the car and my boyfriend tried to go after him. I grabbed him, and when I did, he pushed my arm away. So then my brother and him started to fight. It was a brief tussle and afterwards my brother said to me, "Get your shit and let's go."

So I ran in the house and grabbed what clothes I could and got in the truck. I did not want to leave, but I had to. While we were driving away, my boyfriend aggressively grabbed and jumped on to the passenger door. The kids and I were screaming, I was begging him to let go of the door and he finally jumped off. I had never been so scared in my life. This was a dangerous situation that left me shaking and distressed.

While my brother was driving my children and me to his girlfriend's house, whom was also a good friend of mine, he was cursing and fussing the entire ride. He told me to never go back to him again. Even in that moment, I was trying to figure out how to fix it. Once we arrived and explained what had happened, she so graciously allowed us to stay in her home. My life had gone from calm to chaos in what seemed like a matter of minutes. I could not go back there, although I badly wanted to. *What would life be like without him?*

I had no job or money and I was homeless not knowing what was going to happen with me and the kids. I spent the rest of the night in disbelief, quiet and crying. *How could another man I love do this to me?* The next morning, I woke up in what I hoped was a dream, but it was all a reality. I left everything behind besides what little clothes I grabbed for a few days. It was too much to think about and subconsciously I did not want to believe what had happened.

I was not the type to stay wallowing; I had to gather myself and figure out what steps I needed to take next. *Where and how do I begin?* Life seemed to never work out for me, but one thing was for sure: I needed a plan, but I did not have one.

Picking up the Pieces

It was not always easy for me to pick myself up from a fall, especially after feeling like I was sinking deep into the ocean. I never knew what was next or when the tables would turn, but I did feel overwhelmed after that awful and disastrous day. No matter how strong I pretended to be I was left paralyzed in the moment. I knew life had to go on and it was not going to stop because I wanted it to pause for a minute while I caught my breath. As difficult as this situation was it was time for me to push myself through and get over it.

I called the temporary job agency to make myself available for work again. With tears in my eyes and a broken heart, I still had to figure out my life; I had too much that needed to be done and fast.

The children needed to be transferred to another school. So, I called the elementary school that happened to be directly across the street from my friend's house and asked what I needed to do to transfer my children.

I still had the keys to the townhouse, so I went to get more clothing and personal items the next day while I knew he was at work. The sudden change had me in a fog, but I had to do what needed to be done and stay focus. But every thought of the life I wanted with him while gathering our clothes, made me question myself as a mother. I wanted to have a good life, be a great mom, and do right by my children. Making sure they had what they needed was always priority. I did not know when we would be stable again, but I had to find the energy to make it happen and soon. They did not deserve to be negatively impacted by the unfortunate situation. It was hard for me to believe I had let my children down again, but no matter how difficult things were I was going to move on in a positive way.

I got a call from the agency asking if I was available for a temporary-to-permanent position. The money was not great, but I needed a job… so I accepted. My kids were enrolled in their new school and

I was working, all within the first two weeks of moving.

One lonely evening, I decided to get in touch with my ex-boyfriend because I was missing him so much. He wanted to hurt me more and he did. When I heard the female voice in the background, I knew it was her. It had not taken him long to be back in a rebound relationship with his ex-girlfriend; my heart was crushed.

In a weird and twisted way, when we were together, he made me feel safe from any man hurting me. I felt secure when we were together, although he was possessive. It's what I was missing the most about him. I had been hurt by every man in my life since I was a child and he made me feel protected. *Crazy, right!?*

My father was supposed to be the man who kept me safe but instead, he abandoned me and was in and out of my life—more out than in. Some days I could not think straight. I had allowed myself to be controlled and manipulated by this man, yet I still wanted him and it did not stop me from thinking about him all of the time.

After a couple months on my job, I talked to the rental office where my friend lived, and I applied for a one-bedroom apartment with a den—thank God, I got approved! I had been saving my checks, so I had my rent and security deposit. I was so ready to move in, but I had to work through my insecurities of failing again. I found myself trying to fix the mistakes I kept making over and over again. I had stayed in a toxic relationship with my ex despite the warning signs, it was not enough to make me leave sooner. Of course, I loved my children, but I hated what I had put them through. Whatever troubles I had I tried to hide from them, but sometimes it was impossible for them not to see or hear the complexities of my life. Although, I did not want to admit it I had to be true to myself and accept responsibility for my own actions and stop ignoring the lingering issues from my past.

Keeping secrets and covering up life challenges had become a way of life for me. Staying private about my childhood trauma jump started me into a world of trouble I continued to find myself entangled in. My fear of being alone, rejected, abandoned, or unloved kept me starving for acceptance and seeking validation from bad and toxic relationships.

My life had fallen apart and it was crazy, but we moved in our apartment and that was the first step to restoring my independence. My focus had to be on what was in front of me and not behind me. It was coming together piece by piece and I was making a bad situation better for my children and me. I did not know what was coming down the road or what challenges I would face next, but we have always made it through tough times. Life happens to us all and I was no stranger to disappointment.

CHAPTER 12

MOTHER IN CRISIS

(A Daughter's Love)

Remembrance in life's passing is the truest form of love one can give, for a memory should never die and a love should live forever in the heart of another.
— Laura M. Phipps-Kelley

After coming to terms with the breakup, some unexpected challenges with my mother emerged, as it always did. Her addiction made it nearly impossible for her to provide security and stability in our lives. She was becoming more destructive and complicated and my sister was in the thick of it. When things got out of control and something would happen she or my sister knew to call me for help. I knew I'd get a call from my sister it was inevitable. She depended on me to take care of her during the times our mother failed to.

I never knew if my mother understood just how incomprehensible her addiction was to us. At the end of the day, our love for her was more important, therefore, I had to be a safe place for my mother and be supportive during her struggle with drugs. I'll admit, it was becoming mentally exhausting because the addiction had taken her down a darker path. In truth, she silently battled with her addiction, but regardless of her situation I was not going to let her feel alone I never did and I was not about to start then.

My mother once again needed a place for her and my sister to live. At this point, my sister had been through so many troubled times because of our mother's drug addiction. What once were sporadic drug binges, later turned into more frequent drug use. I had been raised to take care of my mother and siblings and so I did what I had always done without hesitation. So, I picked them up to come stay with me, my mother looked weak and fragile; something here was quite different with her this time. Taking care of only my children and I instantly became less of a priority as I realized in that very moment how deep the problem had affected her life. She was going to be in need of my full attention and I had no idea what all that entailed.

She seemed depressed and less engaging during the drive, saying little to no words at all. I noticed she barely had enough strength to walk to the car. Once we arrived at my apartment, she crawled into bed and I did not know what to do so I let her rest for as long as she needed to. I kept watch over my mom because she literally looked like she was wasting away. Her appetite was poor, only taking a few bites of food, she was tired all of the time, and her energy level was extremely low. This was beyond a mild illness and I had to get her to the hospital. After a few days of only lying around, I asked her if she wanted to go see a doctor. At first, she was hesitant but then said yes. I helped to get her dressed and after arriving at the hospital and being evaluated, she was admitted and they did blood tests and kept her for a couple of days. She definitely was dehydrated, but she seemed to be feeling better after fluids and getting her appetite back.

When she was released from the hospital, I was ecstatic. I saw my mother slowly gaining a little strength back, interacting more in conversations, and spending less time in bed. I kept my eye on her making sure she was taking better care of herself and eating as often as she could, it was not much, but more than before. She had a burst of energy and felt like her old self, then wanted to get out of the house for some fresh air. My mom, sister, and I went out for the day and had the best time; we hadn't had that much fun in a long time! But a couple of days later, she slipped back into a slump again feeling tired and weak, I assumed from our day out. I would come home from work and she would still be in bed and whatever she didn't finish eating was on the floor next to her. That was not like her; anyone who knew her knew how immaculate she kept her living quarters. I was at a loss for words because I could not help her or figure out what was wrong.

I wondered what happened when she was in the hospital, but of course with patient confidentiality and her cognitive ability to make her own decisions, I was not informed of her medical condition or blood test results. My mother was so private and when I'd ask what the doctor said, she'd say, "I'm fine." She wasn't saying much but worry was written all over her face. I knew things were going from bad to worse when she could not make it to the bathroom and was becoming incontinent.

One evening, she called me in the room and I was not expecting what came next. She said, "I think I have AIDS."

I was in shock. "Wait, what did you say?"

My world paused, as I could not believe the words that came out of her mouth. That was the last thing I wanted to hear. *This cannot be happening.* I knew she was sick but for some reason I wasn't thinking it was that form of illness. *How could I hear that and pretend she never said it?*

"Are you sure? Why would you say that?" I asked.

I walked away with tears in my eyes. I closed the bathroom door and cried like a baby. AIDS as I knew it meant one thing: death.

I was not educated on the disease, and I was unsure what to do next. I called my aunt and with tears, I was able to tell her what my mom had said. She was in disbelief while attempting to calm me down. After getting the news, she and her daughter (my cousin) were on their way over. *Did my mother understand what she had said*? I thought about my children and their safety. *What was I going to do?* This was during a time when people thought AIDS could be caught just by being next to an infected person. I was not prepared for the challenge. How could I have been? I did not want to treat my mother like she was the disease. I loved her too much to turn my back on her.

Once my cousin and aunt arrived, we had a talk with my mom, the most challenging yet sobering conversation I'd ever had to have. We knew she needed to go back to the hospital to confirm if what she said was factual. I didn't want to lose my mother; I needed her to be well. I couldn't think about life without her. It was too hard. We managed to get her back to the hospital for more testing. After a couple of days, she was released and yet again did not say anything to us about what the doctor said. While at home, she did not show any signs of improvement. She became more sickly and fatigued by the day. I had to find out what was wrong with her because she looked like she was dying.

The very next morning, I took a chance hoping her doctor would meet with me. I called his office asking if I could talk with him and he agreed, uncertain if he was able to assist me in any way. The many thoughts during the dreadful wait to be called into his office were taking a toll on my mental state. *Please, Lord, do not let it be true!* Once inside the office, "How can I help you?" he asked.

After explaining my mother's condition and what she shared about having AIDS, he looked me in my face and said, "Due to patient confidentiality I cannot release your mom's medical condition to you."

I begged him, explaining that my mom lived with me and I had three small children and her youngest daughter (my sister); if she has AIDS, I needed to know in order to take the proper precautions. With hesitation in his voice and understanding my concerns, he said, "Your mom has full-blown AIDS and it's nothing we can do but make her comfortable. Her T cells, known as white blood cells, were -0 and no medicine would help her. I'm so sorry."

My brain was in overload. I had to process all that was said; it was too much to take in. *Was it true? Maybe he made a mistake. Yeah… it had to have been a mistake.* At least that's what I wanted to believe, but deep down inside I knew what he said was true.

I called my aunt and shared the devastating news and once again they found themselves at my house. I didn't want to have the conversation alone with my mom confirming her status. I will never forget the blank look on her face as I kneeled down holding her hands telling her she had that deadly disease. In that moment, life paused and I didn't quite know how I was going to work through my own thoughts and feelings.

She didn't say a mumbling word. I had to be sure she heard what was said, so I repeated it and her response was, "Okay."

My heart literally broke into a million pieces. *How would we recover?* We could not hold back tears, but she just sat there as if we told her she was healthy and well. We knew we had to get her back to the hospital because I didn't know what to do to take care of her.

I knew the doctor said there was no medication that would help her, but there had to be something. She was skin and bones, and I'm sure dehydrated again because she barely ate or drank much. We got her to the hospital to be examined, she was exhausted and frail. It was becoming a part of my routine and eventually as time progressed, I had to quit my job to be available for what was next in my mother's care. I was the oldest of her children and the responsibility was weighing heavily on me. Thank God, my aunt and cousin were there for me.

After a couple of days in the hospital, decisions needed to be made.

Why? This could not be. It was already one of the worst days of my life already, and the doctor asked me if I wanted my mom to be a "do not resuscitate."

"What are you asking me, doctor? This cannot be real, are you serious?" I asked.

When I thought it couldn't get any worse, the doctor said, "Your mom cannot be released back to your home because she's in need of 24-hour care."

I thought I could provide that for her, so I told the doctor she was coming home with me. "I'm sorry but you cannot provide the care your mom needs," the doctor said.

What a nightmare I was living in. *When was it going to end? None of it seemed to be real.* It was too much to bear and I was not ready to make those decisions. She's my mom. *Please wake me up from this horrendous dream.*

She had to go from the hospital to a skilled nursing facility. This was unchartered territory; my entire life—our life—was changing forever. I was unaware on how to start the process of looking for a nursing home; I just needed my mom to have the best care. It was all happening so fast; my head was spinning. I wanted to escape from what became an instant reality. The doctor said she had only six months or less to live—words no daughter/children ever want to hear.

Our entire world was turned upside down and it just didn't seem right that we had to accept we were losing our mother.

Borrowed Time

After finding what we hoped was the perfect nursing home for our 42-year-old mother dying from AIDS, she was transferred from the hospital to where she would spend her final moments of life. I couldn't understand why this was happening and especially to our family. Life no longer was taken for granted. It makes you want to push the pause button to stop time; because what you have is precious and you need more time to cherish every pivotal moment. Trivial things no longer mattered, you only focus on the present, as time was essential and limited. When you find yourself at a crossroad that you know will break you into pieces, you hope one day you will be able to be put back together. We were left with an enormous hole in our hearts that we knew would forever be with us.

She was too young, and this shouldn't have been her story. I found myself being angry at her, not understanding why we were not good enough reasons to help her make better choices and decisions. *Was I being reasonable?* I had to get back to what was important, and those bitter feelings were not going to change my mom's condition. Knowing you're about to lose your mother was a kind of pain that cripples you, leaving you stuck and unable to move around in life as before, you literally feel handicapped.

Leaving her alone in that nursing home felt wrong, but we were thankful for the staff that provided her with excellent care. My mom had good and bad days, so we made all of the good ones count. We never knew what condition she'd be in because the disease was taking its course. When we laughed, we found everything funny. When we cried, we wanted to find what could make us laugh. But the bad days didn't allow us to be happy, they were overshadowed with sadness. Those days, unfortunately, always seemed like our final moments.

It came time to tell my brother, who at the time was in prison. How do you tell a son who was already in a bad situation that his mom is dying and her final days are getting close? It had to be done and we hoped that we could get a pass for him to visit her one last time. After a few phone calls, the prison approved a visit that allowed him to see our mom.

During one of my visits she said, "I am looking forward to the day my son walks through that door."

It made my heart happy because I knew that day would soon come, and I had to keep the surprise to myself. *Did she have a premonition or something?* Time was moving too fast and we needed it to stop. Having to say goodbye was becoming more apparent. It was obvious she was not going to get better, which broke our hearts repeatedly. We did not want to feel the pain of losing her. I hoped that she would hold on long enough to see her son walk through that door just as she envisioned it.

We told the prison there wasn't much time left; asking them to put a rush on things. They finally were able to give us a date and a time when my brother would be brought to the nursing home.

With much anticipation, the day came. When she looked up, seeing him at that door, her face lit up like lights on a Christmas tree. She said, "Son... son, I knew you would come!"
We all cried and were overwhelmed with joy. We knew that would be the last time he would see her alive. The prison guards had him in a wheelchair, handcuffed and shackled. The excitement that was radiating from my mom and the tears rolling down my brother's face, touched their hearts. He was uncuffed, allowing them time alone as they waited outside the door, and he spent it holding her hand and laying his head on her stomach as she rubbed his head— what an unforgettable moment. He had never seen her like that before; I knew it would break his heart into pieces.

The constant thought of the loss of a mom is gut-wrenching, a feeling that leaves you vulnerable and empty with holes you never think will be filled. We had to prepare our minds and hearts for the day she would take her last breath—the day we would lose her forever. We prayed and believed that God would show mercy and not take her. *Were we being selfish?* Her quality of life had wasted away long before she got to that nursing home, and I remember her previously saying to me, "If I ever get sick and can't take care of myself, do not keep me alive."

She always talked about not wanting to be a burden. Of course, that was crazy talk, but never in a million years did I think we would be faced with that very challenge. My heart was literally breaking, I cried all of the time. I was silently suffering and trying to be strong for my sisters and children. I wanted to change lanes and go in a different direction—*where's the next exit?*

Visits with our mom began to be taxing. We were so afraid as the final months were approaching. The nurse and other staff members became like family and they loved our mom as if she were their own. We never had to worry on the days we couldn't make it to the facility; she was cared for by an amazing group of people.

Death Was Near

On one particular day, it seemed sobering for some reason. My spirit felt heavy, but I thought nothing of it until the phone rang. It was a Friday evening. A call came from the nursing home: "Your mom is not doing good, she slipped into a coma."

Is it happening? My stomach was in knots. I made phone calls to family telling them to get to the nursing home.

You know the day will come, but when it does you tell yourself it's not real. *Please God, don't take our mom, we need her.* She looked so peaceful, but I was not ready to let her go. We all had private time with her to say our goodbyes; I knew she could still hear our voices. "See you later" did not seem so final—I was still in denial. I held her hand and knew I had to say the word "goodbye." I told her if she needed to go that it was okay. I promised her I would take care of my baby sister, her grandchildren, and myself and would keep the promise I made to her to make sure my sister finished high school. It was so difficult verbalizing those words; I wish I never had to say them. To watch the person who carried you for nine months, the one you called "mama," lay helpless and get closer to death was torment.

Staying by her bedside was a must. No one was willing to leave; she was not going to transition alone. While waiting in the room we were having general conversation sharing wonderful memories of my mom with the nurse. All of a sudden, my mother started having convulsions, her eyes rolled in the back of her head, and just like that—no more movement. The room was still for a second until we heard the heart-wrenching scream from my sister and saw her fall to the floor. The nurse checked for a pulse and with tears in her eyes said, "I'm sorry, she is gone."

Loudly I said, "No!" and went running down the hall.

It was the worst few minutes of our lives. My family was in an uproar! *This is not how she was supposed to die. God, why?*

My cousin came after me saying, "She's back. She has a pulse!"

Relieved and frightened, I walked back into the room. My mom was peacefully lying there as if nothing ever happened. I hugged my children, sister, and other family members tightly. It was too much. My heart was beating what seemed like 100 MPH. *What was God up to?* We appreciated the extra time He gave us and without reservation we held onto every breath she took.

Rotating shifts is what we did the entire weekend so she wouldn't be by herself. On that beautiful, sunny, fall Saturday morning, we cracked her window a little to allow some fresh air to flow through her room. She shocked us all and opened her eyes, we all surrounded her bed wanting to ask a million questions, but we knew she was too weak to utter a word—or, so we thought. Softly she said, "I'm thirsty."

We quickly got the nurse. She checked her vitals and was as shocked as we were. My mother sipped juice through a straw like she was literally dying of thirst. Her raspy whispered words could barely be heard; we didn't care, we were just happy to hear her speak, hoping it wouldn't be the last time. She was back and we were enjoying the moment. No one wanted to leave her side, not even to use the bathroom. The woman I thought was invincible was not and we were left waiting for her to die, I was not going to be okay.

As the evening went by, we noticed her eyes closed and opened, closed and opened, closed and she was peaceful again. I didn't think of that being the last time I would ever look into her eyes. We were tired but afraid to sleep not wanting to wake up to her being gone. We'd hoped things would change and her beautiful brown eyes would open again, but they did not.

On Sunday night, my cousin took my sister and children home while my aunt and I stayed by her bedside. I watched my mom and I knew death was near. We couldn't really sleep; we were still up when the birds starting chirping and the sun began to rise. The nurse came to examine her and said, "It's close. She barely has a pulse. We need to call hospice."

When the hospice nurse finally arrived, she asked us to step out of the room; within a few minutes she was done and while I sat in the chair, she gave me a kiss on my forehead saying, "God bless you and your family" as she walked away.

I was confused as to what just happened. I pulled the curtain back to go in with my mom and I witnessed her as she took her last and final breath; she was gone. I calmly got the nurse and hoped I was wrong, but she confirmed and pronounced my mother deceased on September 23, 1996, at 8:05 a.m.

A Special Tribute

Jeanette Wilkins-Kennedy (5-7-54 to 9-23-96)

Jeanette was a mother, grandmother, sister, aunt, cousin, and friend and we all loved her so much and will always remember her infectious smile, strength during her weakest times, and the love she had for her children, grandchildren, and family. Our mother's love did not die with her it's not buried in the grave, but her love lives forever in our hearts. We miss her still today, think of her often, and daydream about what life could have been. Thank you, mother, for watching over all of us you left behind. We know you did not want to leave, but you had to go.

We miss you on Earth, but we know you are rejoicing in heaven and knowing that you are healed from all pain, sorrow, sickness, disease, and suffering is how we get through some of our most challenging moments without you. You gave us life and we are living it to our fullest potential with thoughts of you every step of the way. We thank God for the time he gave us with you! It was a gift that we treasured and honored. Until we meet again, continue to rest eternally in his arms.

Never forget those who lost their lives to AIDS and the ones who are still fighting the good fight and living with HIV/AIDS. I stand with you, we stand with you, as we continuing to pray for a cure that will one day save your life and the lives of our family and friends.

My beautiful mother, but somebody said something she didn't like lol.

Always had a big beautiful smile.

I miss my momma.

Me and my mother looking like twins.

Her smile was contagious.

One of the saddest days of my life was the day I loss my mother.

THE UNVEILING

CHAPTER 13
MANY CHALLENGING MOMENTS

(Life Was Different)

Life Has Many Ways Of Testing A Person's Will, Either By Having Nothing Happen At All Or By Having Everything Happen All At Once.
—Paulo Coelho

After the funeral, I didn't know what I was going to do without my mother. I wanted to numb the pain but how and with what? "I wish I could have saved her," is what I told myself over and over.

I believed I failed her and could have done more; I did not try hard enough. The guilt was heavy; I do not recall a day going by without crying and asking why.

We do not get to choose our parents and by no means was our mother perfect, but we loved her dearly. My thoughts about what she must have been going through that led her to drugs haunted me even more. Sharing her pain and hurt was not her strong suit. I wish she would have verbalized and released what she was keeping inside. Nonetheless, she was gone, and we had to wrestle with that unimaginable and heartbreaking loss.

I was back in a relationship with my ex-boyfriend, and he attempted to comfort me as much as he could. I tried to escape the pain of losing my mother by spending more time with him and less time at home where I was forced to face the loss. I needed to be the shoulder my sister and kids leaned on, instead I was running away from the truth. I felt the absence of her every day and I could barely ease my pain, let alone theirs. Nighttime was more challenging; I did not want to sleep because dreaming and seeing her face reminded me of the reality of her death. Life without her already felt empty and I was not as prepared as I thought I was.

She was gone and that was very hard to accept. I knew I had to live but how could it even be possible? The air smelled different, the sun shined dimmer, the stars weren't as bright, and the clouds seemed darker. Everything around me was not the same and I had to learn how to cope with life in a way I never had to before. No matter the struggles my mother had, I always knew she loved us as best as she knew how, and we loved her back. In the days and weeks that followed her death, feeling anything but anger only seemed right. I cried most days until my head was pounding and I could barely breathe. Even if for a second, minute, or an hour I just wanted to forget she was gone. *God why did you take her? Why didn't you heal her?* I wanted Him to bring her back to us! Please don't let somebody say, "God picked a rose," I was not ready to hear those words.

Back To The Old

My boyfriend and I were rebuilding our relationship, which took my mind off of the death of my mother temporarily. I never stopped loving him, so it was easy to pick up the broken pieces of our relationship and mend them back together. I forgave him because he deserved another chance. He seemed different—maybe he was being sensitive to the loss of my mother—whatever it was, I did not want it to end. My heart was so torn between the past and the present, but I was determined to make my second chance with him better than before. I wanted to be the center of his world. I wanted forever with him, hoping nothing came between us. For some reason, I made myself believe I could not live without him.

I couldn't forget my responsibilities and the promise to my mother to make sure my sister finished high school. I was becoming so consumed with making him happy that I lost sight of my duties at home. I was overlooking signs and red flags, not noticing he was monopolizing all of my time. I took a deep breath and realized I needed to be more present at home. He wanted to be wherever I was, so he made staying home easier to manage. For one thing, I was not the only one who lost a mother, my sister did too and she was hurting. She was young, her pain was expressed differently and I was fully aware that her hurt was deeper than I could have ever imagined.

My boyfriend helped me with things that she needed, which made me love and depend on him more. He called her his little sis. I was her sister and mother. She was starting to like boys, and there was one in particular that she would talk to me about. I tried not to be an overbearing big sister, but I wanted to tell her she was too young to date. I wanted to protect her from the same mistakes that I had made.

We were making the best out of our new norm and weren't happy about it, but we knew life had to go on. We were just figuring out how to live without our mother. Our other sister was living her own life apart from us and we barely saw or heard from her, and our brother was still in prison. We had each other to share our grief with and it was hard most days.

As difficult as life was, we decided to move from the house we were in, it was best for us to move away and start fresh. I knew I couldn't afford anything of luxury, but I did find us another house. Once we moved into our new place, I started seeing the boy whom my sister talked a lot about more and more. I didn't give it too much thought, my boyfriend became my distraction, and I was trying to cater to his needs while neglecting my own. I was twenty-four years old, and I was losing control and everything started to be an unbearable burden. My sister's challenges became my challenges, my children were clingier and I was reaching a breaking point. My grief was tearing me apart; it was causing havoc in my world and all I wanted was to see my momma again.

Toxic Love

My relationship was starting to fall to pieces, and I was standing face to face with his controlling, possessive, aggressive, and jealous ways. *This cannot be happening again.* It was like a switch turned on. I began to question myself about being back with him, but I wanted us to work. Living my life with him was what I wanted so badly, so every sorry was accepted, all hugs were embraced, and every gift after an argument was gracefully received. Each time was a new day, another start, followed by "I love you so much." It was sweet melodies to my ears. I loved him and did not have the energy to keep arguing, so my excusing his behavior became easier than forcing him to change. All the good he had in him outweighed every uncomfortable feeling I had staying in the relationship.

He loved my children and sister so much and anything I needed or wanted, he provided. My focus needed to be on my sister and children, but I didn't want to cheat him of my time either. *How long could I live like this?* It was so unhealthy. I was emotionally, physically, and mentally exhausted; I had no more fight left in me to maintain this relationship. But I couldn't handle another loss; it was too soon after losing my mother. I was not ready to let go of him too.

I did all I could to overlook and excuse his behavior. He wanted to be first and I did not know how to give him that especially when I had other responsibilities. I knew I wanted to be the apple of his eye, but I had no idea how to make him see me. I had been in a marriage with a man who said he loved me and treated me like I was easily replaceable, which I was. My self-esteem was low and although I was overwhelmed in this relationship, I couldn't muster up enough strength to walk away. So, I continued to stay giving him more power and control.

As time went on, he got worse. He became more jealous, needing to know my whereabouts and whom I was spending my time with. He drove through the back alley of my house with his headlights off to catch me allegedly cheating and tracking my every move. Accusing me of things I wasn't doing. His paranoia was at an all-time high, and I felt stuck in the unhealthy relationship. I loved this man, seemingly more than myself, but I could not help him. There was nothing I could do to fix it anymore. I was tired. And he was making it easier not to stay. Despite his possessive and intimidating ways, he had a softer side to him… but his jealousy was disturbing. I knew I needed to disconnect from him because I had enough of it. He was bringing out the worst parts of me and it was ugly. I had just loss my mother and recently found out my sister was pregnant— he forgot about all I was dealing with. He wanted everything to be about him. Anger and bitterness had taken its toll on me; my happiness was obsolete. I felt guilty for wanting to leave him, but I needed a way out of the situation!

One morning, we got into an argument that resulted in him yanking the telephone from the wall and busting out the windshield in the car that he bought me. That should have been enough for me to finally have enough, right? *Nope!* I could not explain this inexplicable desire to still want to be with him after what he had done.

He called and apologized later that night asking if he could pick me up, and my heart and mouth said yes before I could allow my mind to say no. He made me forget all about what happened, as he usually did. Apologizing over and over again! The next morning, I felt foolish, but he said he was sorry; and offered to pay to get my window repaired. I told myself he didn't really mean it and brushed it off. I wanted to live life with this man, but at what cost? What was I willing to give up, or had I already done that? I knew I never should have gone back to him; I was spending my time trying to prove my worth. The stress was boiling, and I was about to explode.

My sister needed me more than ever and I didn't want her to bear the responsibility by herself or feel alone. I had to be by her side, but instead I was constantly reassuring my boyfriend that he could trust me. I had too much on my already full plate and it was taking a toll on my heart and my emotions. I was barely holding on by a thread and trying to keep it together. I had not fully dealt with my grief; I was feeling so much heartache at once.

Finding out my sister was further along in her pregnancy than I expected made it so surreal. Being there for my sister, my children, and my boyfriend's needs were overwhelming. I had to keep pushing with what little determination I had left. He wasn't making my load lighter. I tried so many times to give him a fair chance and not walk away, but it was not worth my time and energy anymore. I had to get away from him, but I couldn't do it with my own strength. I just could not deal with the stories he believed in his head about me that were not happening. So, I did what was best and I got on my knees and I prayed, "Lord, I love this man, but I cannot take this anymore. Please remove him from my life without killing him."

After I prayed, I was not even sure I really wanted him out of my life. I was in love, but I was tired of all the chaos and back and forth nonsense. I was still grieving my mother and he would not even give me space to do that.

Later on that evening, a loud knock at my door startled me, it was one of his good friends. My boyfriend had gotten into some trouble that caused him to get hurt. He was taken to the hospital and nearly lost his life—thank God, he survived. I was so scared and only wanted him to be okay. He was in the hospital for a couple of weeks recovering from his injuries. I was devastated at how I almost lost him for good. I could not leave him as I wanted to so I stood by his side as any good woman would. Before being transferred to prison after being accused of an alleged crime, I knew giving up on him was not an option. He needed me, and I felt indebted to him. He had stuck by my side through many things, and I believed he deserved me being by his side.

Months went by, and the news from his lawyer was not getting any better, only worse. We were hoping he'd come home soon, but it was not looking as though he was. The lawyer prepared us for court and after several hearings the verdict came: "Guilty."

This cannot be happening. I was hoping for a better outcome, wishing we could go back in time. Although we had this tumultuous relationship, it didn't define my love for him. *What was I going to do without him?* I was reminded of the prayer to remove him from my life. *Oh Lord, was all of this my fault?*

I felt guilty about the trouble he was in as if I caused it. He had a way of making me believe I did something wrong to him without saying a word. I wanted to support him, so I continued to visit him every chance I got, no matter the cost. Even while he was behind bars I was accused of cheating, I tried to consider his feelings and be understanding. But his jealousy would rear its ugly head even behind the glass that separated us. After he denied my visits a couple of times pushing me further away from his life, I stopped going to see him and I knew I had to make some changes. I could no longer ignore the truth that I felt like I was being held hostage in the relationship. Our relationship was toxic and had been from the beginning. But my love for him had clouded my judgment and I constantly ignored all the fed flags that were being waved in my face. I wrestled with him not being around and I still loved him no matter what.

What Was I Going to Do Now?

As the months passed, I felt alone. I missed him so much and I cried a lot. I stayed in contact with his family, which didn't make it easy to move on from the situation and put him behind me. He made several attempts to call me, and we chatted some, but I knew it was over. Although he made my life miserable at times, he had always made sure we had what we needed. Life for me was starting to look a little dimmer; the struggle was real. I wasn't working, and we were living off of limited income and resources. I was doing my best to stay afloat. Unfortunately, trying to stay caught up on bills continued to fail and I knew I had to do something. Not only was I responsible for my three sons and sister, but another life was going to be born and added to that list soon. I had always figured our way out of tight spots, but for some reason I felt closed in with no way out. It was hard without him because he had made life financially easier for me, but without him I was struggling to put food on the table.

I was losing my mind, but my sister always had a way of cheering me up simply by being there and telling me, "We are in this together."

And we were.

I wanted her to be proud of me, and to be honest I was disappointed in myself. It seemed as if I was letting her and my children down, but I was doing the best with what I had. I could not give up, although that didn't seem like a bad idea; I wholeheartedly wanted to break down and cry. I just didn't want to do life anymore!

We thought about our mother so much and the first few holidays without her were some of the toughest times. Missing her was painful and we leaned on one another for comfort as often as we could; it was almost impossible to push through the hurt. We were struggling with our emotions. Our mother should have been with us, but instead she was gone.

My sister looked up to me; I had to be the stronger one and I tried everything I could to be in a happy place in my life with all the sadness around me, but it was easier said than done.

I became so angry. I wasn't grieving as I wanted to and losing my mother changed my life forever. Kicking, screaming, punching a hole in a wall, crying were all things I wanted to do, but I couldn't. I had three little people and my sister who was just as hurt over the death of my mother and none of us had even began to heal. I was expected to act a certain way, but at times I did not know what to really do to comfort them. I was grief stricken, but who was going to help pick me up while I was down? God knew I needed His strength if I was going to live and not crawl under a rock and die! There were days I didn't want to breathe, laugh, think, or feel; I just wanted to be left alone.

The Unthinkable

After everything I was already dealing with, one day my 7- and 9-year-old sons did not come home from school. I gave them a few extra minutes, thinking they were goofing off with friends. Those minutes felt like hours, so I went looking for them at the school and they were not there. Trying not to panic, I started looking around the neighborhood and asking if anyone had seen them. We didn't live in the best part of town, and I was becoming more and more concerned about their whereabouts.

It was cold outside and got dark early and there was no sign of my babies. They were not familiar with the city yet, so I thought the worst: *Somebody kidnapped my boys.* That was the only thing that made sense at the time. The tears were flowing, my heart was beating faster, and I became more afraid than I had ever been in my life.

I called the police to report them missing and my family rushed over for support. Describing my kids, what they had on, and when I saw them last was a feeling of hopelessness and despair. On top of walking around showing their pictures and asking the question, "Have you seen them?"

The no's were like sharp needles poking at my heart. Hour after hour with no signs of them in sight, I began to think somebody had hurt my children; I didn't want to believe my own thoughts. *God you cannot be doing this to me.* A mother's worst nightmare is the loss of not one, but two, children. *Where are my babies? How could this be happening?* I tried to stay positive but the later it got the more discouraged I became. The unimaginable raced to the front of my mind. I tried to hold it together, but I was breaking and falling apart not knowing if I would ever see them again. I felt like I was in a scary movie afraid to face the monster I was hiding from. I didn't want to come out in a world my children no longer existed in.

I went off alone to pray, "Lord, please bring my children home to me. Please let them be all right. I beg of you Lord, bring them home to me; I need my children to be safe."

Soon after, the police knocked on the door. It was close to midnight. "I think we found your children and they are safe."

With praises and tears in my eyes, I asked, "Where are they?"

"Another officer is with them. They were found at the inner harbor after a security officer spotted them with another little boy swinging on the ropes over the water. Security got them into his office. They were cold and hungry."

I just wanted them home; I could not have been more excited about knowing they were alive and well!

When the officer brought them home and they walked through that front door, my family and I grabbed, hugged, and squeezed them so tight. I never wanted to let them go. In that very moment, I didn't care about the what, why, when, or how—I saved it for the next day.

The next morning, I learned the other little boy asked my sons to go with him and they agreed. They were walking and following the other kid who led them down to the Baltimore Inner Harbor. Living in the city and seeing young kids on their own was not uncommon, so it was easy for people to overlook what was normal. After hearing their story, I was mad because it could have ended another way and they knew better than to do anything other than come straight home from school. As overjoyed as I was, because my babies were home safe and sound, I couldn't help but think, what if. I never wanted to experience anything like that ever again in life; no mother should.

Feeling Overwhelmed

Life was suffocating me, and I felt heavily weighed down. I didn't know what to do anymore; nothing felt right. I felt like I was headed down a rabbit hole, I was miserable, and I desperately wanted to escape it. I was emotionally cracking into little pieces becoming more uncertain of the days ahead. Feeling trapped inside of my pain, hurt, and anger made me feel worthless and defeated. So many decisions had to be made and I was just not up to making any of them. I always had to remain the strong one, but I was depressed and carrying around so much heaviness on the inside. Sometimes you look at life and wonder how you got to the place you can't seem to move away from. Someone in my situation would have given up, and trust me, I thought about it more often than I should have. I wanted to be the hero everyone saw me as, however my superwoman cape was full of holes, and I was flying low.

It was getting closer to the time for my sister to have the baby and I was still stuck in my own fears and anxiety. I thought I could be everything she needed me to be, and I was doing my best to make things happen. I tried to provide the stability she never had from our mother and at times I felt no different. She and my children loved me and counted on me to help conquer their fears, yet I was drowning in my own. It had only been a little less than a year since my mother's death and I was forcing myself through the grief process. Losing her had a death grip on me and I was sinking deeper into depression that no one saw. The lights were out emotionally, it was getting the best of me and yet I was left with figuring out our next situation during one the darkest times in my life.

Trying to Make it

We lived in a two-bedroom house, which was barely enough space for the five of us. I knew we at least needed a three-bedroom house. We were moving more frequently than what I wanted us to; it seemed like every six months. No matter what I was going through, I had to find us more space before the baby was born and searching for another place to move was not only about the size, but the location and price.

After looking at a few places, I finally found a really nice three-bedroom townhouse in a much better community and neighborhood. I wondered how we would make it, I knew I couldn't afford that place, but I was not going to turn it down. We had no choice but to move. I was always finding myself robbing Peter to pay Paul—never having enough income to pay my bills, struggling to just keep a roof over our head, lights on, and food in the fridge. Being in the new place would be no different.

There were many days I cried when no one was looking. Financial hardship had been a close companion of mine; I saw no way out of the crisis in the near future. I was dragging along, slowly putting one foot in front of the other. Bills, children's expenses, and so many problems were a never-ending story. I was not sure how I was going to handle it all, but I was used to life being hard.

We had been in our new townhouse for several months and already we were experiencing financial difficulties and struggled to pay the rent. This time it was different because we were only days away from my sister's due date and the rent needed paid. The rent was due, and I had to speak with the rental office and practically beg for an extension, which I prayed they'd honor. They granted us the extension and I had a couple of weeks to get the remaining balance. I knew I was getting another paycheck that would cover what we needed; even though we would have the same problem the next month. But, *One thing at a time*, is what I told myself.

A good friend of mine had told me about some low-income townhouses that only went by your income and she thought I should apply and put my name on their waiting list and for the heck of it, so I did! I knew it was a long shot and it would be years, but it was still worth the try. God knows I would love to have something like that, but what are the chances of that really happening?

It was a hot, sunny day and my sister had an appointment we needed to get to. I had been pushing myself to get through all of what I was dealing with and it was time to turn my attention elsewhere.

After my sister's doctor appointment, later that day she felt some discomfort that would not go away. Several hours had gone by and she was feeling the pressure of what could possibly be labor. She wasn't sure if they were actual contractions, but we headed to the hospital after the apparent labor pains became more regular and stronger. I was there every step of the way. It was really happening—my sister was about to have a baby! New life was entering the world and into our family and just like that… a healthy baby boy was born.

I was now responsible for so much more and I did my best, even though I felt it was never good enough. I was still feeling the pain of losing my mother, we both were. All of these different emotions at once, if ever a time it was then to pick up the pieces of my broken heart and start to heal. It would be hard, and I knew that, our mother was gone, but I had to tend to my sister, children, and now nephew. Although we felt incomplete, the new addition made us feel so much better, soothing the pain, but at the end of day we knew our mother was still gone.

With the joys of the baby, I didn't forget the other portion of the rent was still due and now the current months was too. I was definitely tired of struggling, it became immobilizing. But I tried to keep my faith and trusted God to come through for us as He had so many times before. It was difficult and challenging because I did waver in my faith. I couldn't understand why there was so much pain in my life all of the time. It was constant. I wasn't sure if God's promises were for me any longer. I had become used to always being in survival mode and it was sucking the life out of me. I never made too much of a big deal about struggling to family or friends, I kept a lot of it to myself or shared with my sister. I was tripping and falling all throughout life and this financial burden remained a continuous nagging problem that wouldn't go away. As a result, I wasn't so sure how I was going to keep juggling in the tough times. With all things considered, I had to ensure myself that one day things will get easier. In the meantime, I had to take each day as it came!

CHAPTER 14

GOOD AND BAD DAYS

(Finally, some Breaks)

Never regret a day in your life. Good days give you happiness, bad days give you experience, worst days give you lessons, and best days give you memories.
—Inspirational Quotes Journal

Making ends meet was becoming harder month after month; always choosing which bill was more important to pay than others. It was difficult staying ahead and trying to keep up, I thought I wasn't going to make it, but somehow I knew I had no choice… we could not be homeless. I would pay the rent before the eviction date, but I knew that there was no way they were going to renew my lease; I wasn't their ideal tenant. I was thankful for payment extensions, because without it we would have seen many more dark days. There was a stack of bills that needed to be paid and I was not catching up on them any time soon. I felt like I was constantly treading water and trying to make it with what little I had.

I was not expecting to get a phone call so soon about the low-income housing, but it was a call I was grateful for. When the lady said that my name had reached the top of the list and asked if I was still interested, of course I said, "Yes!"

After hanging up the phone, my heart skipped a few beats from all of the joy and excitement! I assumed it would have been years that I'd be on that housing list. I told my sister about the phone call, we were so happy, jumping up and down, thanking God. It was what we so desperately needed. But all of the enthusiasm came to a halt when the phone rang again. The same lady called back to apologize, saying that she had made a mistake—There was one name ahead of mine. I think I was so used to hard times all I could say was, "Thank you, no problem."

You could feel the sadness in the room. It was quiet for a moment, "Well, at least we will be next on the list," I said out loud to my sister."

We were so disappointed!

Nearly an hour later, the phone rang again, and it was the same lady calling back. She said that the other person ahead of me could not accept the offer due to a family illness. Although I was not happy about what that other family was experiencing, I was glad to have this chance. I asked her to reassure me it was real that time, and she did.

We were moving to Columbia, Maryland, and I couldn't have been more ready for the financial breakthrough! After arranging a day and time to meet the housing lady, I tried to remain calm until afterwards. I was afraid of something going terribly wrong, as it always did. At the appointment, I found out my rent was going to be $62 for a four-bedroom, two-bath townhouse. I wanted to hug her, do back flips, and scream, "Thank you Jesus!"

Wait, are you serious? I thought it was a joke until I signed the leasing agreement.

When you have been down for so long, it's hard to believe you can look up safely with confidence. We were ready for a change. I had given my all with what we had, there was nothing left. Packing never felt so good, again, I was thankful to God for it. There were so many days and nights I longed to be in a better place, our life was filled with all sorts of ups and downs. We had more than our fair share of challenges and we were hoping just for a little ray of sunshine to stay with us longer than a hot minute.

We moved in the first few days after the New Year of 1998. It was so spacious with three levels—just what we needed. We stayed up all that night until every piece of furniture was in its place. I think the adrenaline from all the excitement fueled our energy. We walked through our new home amazed at every room, the space, and how affordable it was, which was the best part of the move. You couldn't imagine the joy we felt being nearly evicted. Yet we kept going, hoping, wishing, and praying that tomorrow would be the day that things would change. I didn't expect for it not to be hard, I just wanted life to be easier.

On Monday morning, it was time to register the kids and my sister into their new schools. The cold air smelled so fresh and the walk to the school was filled with conversation, laughter, observing, and a peace of mind… I was so relieved. I wanted to hold on to that feeling and not let go. It was winter, but that day seemed warmer than usual. It was as if a ton of bricks had been lifted off my shoulders and I finally had room to breathe.

Once everyone was in school and meeting new friends, we became accustomed to the surrounding area and neighborhood. We were within walking distance to shopping centers, the mall, restaurants, and supermarkets. I did not have a car at the time, so the nearby places were convenient. The environment was different from what we were used to, but we adapted. We quickly introduced ourselves and become friendly with our neighbors. We just wanted to feel welcomed in the community and soon we were meeting even more new people. Everything seemed to be going well and I expected someone to wake me up from what felt like a dream. My brain wanted to relax, but my thoughts were scattered. I was so used to failing that I thought about all of the reasons things could go wrong. The conversations I had with myself reassured me that things were not perfect, but they were better. I had gone through and was still facing so much inner turmoil. So, the best thing I could do was stop worrying about something bad happening and enjoy our new beginning.

Advantages and Disadvantages

I had the opportunity through a temporary job agency to work in a correctional facility, which was a long-term position. I accepted the offer because I needed a job, and the hours were perfect, and the pay was not that bad. After working there for almost a year, I was asked to be a permanent employee. The details of my job and hours would change drastically. The mother of a friend of mine was the director of corrections and she was able to offer me a full-time job as a correctional officer. Now this job offer would change our life and I was delighted to say, "Yes."

After going through their new hire process and being accepted for the job, I had to go to the academy training. After successfully completing it, I was placed on the night-shift position from 11 p.m. to 7 a.m. I wasn't thrilled about that part, but I had to start there as a new officer.

Truth is that life started looking up for us and I was bringing home money I had never made before. After notifying the housing company of my new earnings my rent was raised tremendously, but it was still affordable. For the first time, it felt good not to struggle and worry about how we were going to make it. When you have spent your life not being able to provide everything for your children, the excitement of having the means to afford a life of security and stability put me in a good place emotionally. My financial stress were burdens that were lifted in midair and I was floating. Moving on from my struggles was quite freeing and all I wanted was to keep progressing forward to a life I had only imagined before then. I was far from rich, but we were living a pretty darn good life.

Our day to day was not perfect, my sister and I had many setbacks and struggles but through it all we remained stronger because of it. We found that we could get through anything as long as we were together. So far things were still going good and I had my sight on something I wanted for myself. One day, I went to the car dealer and was able to purchase a brand-new car for the first time in my life. I never thought it was possible for me to do, but I was financially stabled and had the funds. There was nothing wrong with me being truly happy about getting a new car, although I almost talked myself out of doing it. I deserved to have this—I was working hard and had sacrificed so much. It was my time to shine bright like a diamond. I had my fair share of walking, catching buses, cabs, and driving a lemon.

I loved my job and the money because it was providing my family exactly what we needed. There were so many things that were putting a smile on my face other than my job, car, and financial security. I was gaining the attention from a few male correctional and police officers. I was flattered by all of the flirting and compliments. From one officer to another, they would tell me how beautiful and sexy I was. I knew they were only after one thing, but it was still impressive, and I didn't mind hearing it. I had some lonely nights and was still missing my ex-boyfriend who had been locked up for almost two years. I had dated a few guys here and there, but nothing too serious so I was available for some fun adult time. As we all know, that can get out of hand and things can end up going good or bad.

As a result, I ended up in a relationship with a man I worked with. I really liked him, as he did me. Our feelings grew quickly for one another, but I had problems committing. I had been through too much to fully trust that a man could love me or be honest. And although I was a single woman, I was also a single mother of three boys and not yet ready to involve a man in their lives. I didn't want to waste my time or his. I was interested, but not ready to settle down. After a few months, I put an end to our relationship, calling it off for good. I could only give him pieces of me, but he wanted the whole pie.

Working together was not easy since it was obvious we had feelings for one another. We remained cordial at the workplace and at times I wanted to try with him again, but it was best we stayed strictly friends. I continued to casually date when I had time, but no one seemed to grab my attention long enough to love them. I was so over relationships, men, and dating, but I was hopeful to real love finding its way to me one day.

Trying to Figure it all Out

I just needed time to think about what I needed in my life. I thought I was in a better place emotionally, however, I started developing these unexplained feelings of not knowing where, or with whom, I belonged. I felt I wanted to do more, but I didn't have a clue what that looked liked. I was feeling lost and didn't know why… it was weird because I thought I was happy.

I needed some space and distance between my past disappointments and the dangers of my then present thoughts. My thinking was not the same as my desires and I wasn't connecting with myself as I once was. Nothing was feeling the same anymore. I went from being thrilled about my job, finances, new car, and hoping one day to find love to becoming angry. I started feeling guilty about the life I had created as if I did not deserve it. I was denying myself the right to feel good about feeling so good.

We often sabotage our lives out of fear of the unknown. These emotions did not make any sense and certainly there was no clear explanation about the concerns I was suddenly experiencing.

For years, I lived a life that others had created for me, and I wasn't sure if I was living my true desires or someone else's. Did I really know what I wanted or was I just following along with the things I thought I should be doing? I built this new life pretending having enough money and fewer struggles would make everything alright. To be honest, I attached myself to things I never had, but I was not used to any of what I had and it was causing me anxiety with the thoughts of losing it all.

It seemed I was more comfortable having little than I was with having more. It was easier not to be loved than to have someone love me. Being down was better than being up because I was familiar there. I was struggling to break free from a poverty mentality, therefore when I had a hundred dollars, I treated it like ten dollars. Although my income changed, I still felt insignificant and limited on the things I should have. In the midst of this complicated finding of myself, I was mentally all over the place trying to figure it all out. It may have taken some time, but deep inside I knew I'd rather be living a satisfied and fulfilled life and not a life of flounder. There were still parts of me I couldn't get to the bottom of, but I didn't want to regret the things in which I had accomplished or be scared to embrace it.

<u>Crisscross</u>

One day while visiting a family member, I met a young man. He was handsome and grabbed my attention the second I laid eyes on him. It didn't take him long to call me over and ask for my number, which I gladly gave him. He called the same night and we talked for hours. We seemed to share some common interests, and he fed my ego telling me what I wanted to hear.

One day, I picked him up and we went back to my house. At first, we talked a while, but then I realized taking him to my bedroom wasn't a good idea. I tried avoiding being intimate with him, but neither of us controlled our desire for it. Afterward, I thought, *Not again with someone I do not want*. When it was time for him to leave something clicked in my mind, *Wait, I have to drive him back home!* He didn't have a car. For a moment I was so caught up that I forget that small detail. I knew it wouldn't be long before I ended whatever it was with him, he had nothing to offer or add to my life. It was over sooner than I could blink… I did not have time to waste.

After one week of us not talking, I decided to give him a call. I'm not sure why, but I did. He was not home, but his cousin that I had met once or twice before was there. After telling me he was not there, he was polite by saying, "Hello, remember me, how have you been?"

That led to more questions that turned into a long conversation about life, children, family, and goals. He did not hold back making sure I knew his cousin was seeing other people while he was seeing me. Do not get me wrong, I was glad that brief fling was over, but how could he?

Before hanging up he asked if he could call me sometimes as a friend. I assumed it was innocent—*what harm could it be?* So, I agreed. He seemed to be a really nice guy. I realized we were talking almost daily for about a week before he asked to take me out on a date. His confession of liking me was flattering, but he was not who I would usually be attracted to—but did I really have a type?

The night we were supposed to go out was interrupted. Something came up for him, but he bought me flowers, which was sweet, and we made plans to reschedule. We continued talking on the phone and I wasn't sure where the conversations were leading to, but he told me he wanted more and hoped I did too. It was something I needed to think about because I only saw him as a good friend, but I always enjoyed talking to him. He brightened my days, especially after working all night. I loved the fact that he was a single dad of two little girls, 3 and 5 years old. That was honorable and attractive to me.

On one particular day, he did not call me. Yes, I noticed because I was used to him checking on me daily at that point. I called him and instead I received some devastating news from his brother.

The Flip Side of Things

His brother told me that he had been assaulted—beaten with a baseball bat nearly to death. He was in the hospital in the trauma unit fighting for his life and was in a medically induced coma.

My heart dropped. After hearing the news, I felt a sense of grief and sorrow and was at a loss for words. My first reaction was I wanted to see him, but he was not allowed visitors other than family. As the days went on, I called his mom daily to check on him. She appreciated me caring about her son.

One day, she asked if I wanted to visit. It was an honor and my pleasure. Once we arrived, I was a little shaken up, being uncertain of what I would see. I became tearful looking at him and got closer with the permission of his mom. I held his hand and began softly speaking to him. I said his name and told him he would be alright. To his mom's and my surprise, he slightly opened his eyes and with a raspy whisper he said my name, then went back to being unresponsive. His mom looked at me while placing her hands over her mouth and with tears in her eyes said, "You are the first and only person he has responded to."

I did not know how to feel about that, but my heart fluttered with a sense of peace and connection to this man—*but why, though?* I thought of him often and stayed in touch with his mom concerning his condition. I could not stop thinking about him or the image of seeing him in such a badly beaten state.

When he finally woke up from the medically induced coma, his mom called me saying he asked about me. She suggested I go to see him, knowing that would make his day. I saw him a couple of times before he was transferred to rehab. He needed extensive therapy as his jaw was wired shut with metal plates too, and he had to learn to walk steadily again. I visited him at the rehabilitation center on my days off from work and I could tell he was falling in love with me by the way he looked at me. When he was discharged, I saw him more frequently and I too began to develop these unprecedented feelings. I tried to pretend it was not real. I had never liked someone like him before. He was as skinny as a stick; mouth wired shut, face sunken in, no job, money, or car. He literally had nothing that should have attracted me to him in any way. But he admired me so much, calling me his angel. I did not expect to care for him in the way that I did.

He would ask me to stop over to his place on my way to work because he had cooked me food for the night. Every morning, we would pray together, and he always reminded me that I was his angel and I was the reason he was getting better. He treated me like a queen, making sure I knew my worth and how special I was to him. I was so infatuated by the treatment that I started to find him more attractive and charming. I was so out of my comfort zone and wasn't quite sure how to make sense of these feelings, but I just went with it. He wanted me to be his girlfriend, and truthfully, I wanted to. The first time he kissed me, he was afraid of how I would respond. I could see the nervousness, but I kissed him back. Soon after, we became romantically involved, making our relationship official. Love came in a strange way and at an unexpected time, but it happened and I was not letting it pass me by.

Now it was time to introduce him to my family. I was invested in getting to know him and his young daughters more, seeing anybody else was not an option. I was committed to spending as much time as I could with him and enjoying every minute of it. When my sister met him for the first time she was confused as to my intentions with this man and why I was with him, she said it had to be out of pity. He was not that easy on the eyes, but he melted my heart and I wanted him just as much as he wanted me. He had nothing financially to offer me, but he was exactly what I needed. His love for me meant more to me than his looks or money! He was extremely nice to my boys, playing and spending quality time with them, and that made them like him even more because he was fun. Our children got along most of the time despite the age and gender difference. My heart was starting to soften more for him; I was falling deeply in love. I accepted the life I was having with him although my family questioned and did not understand it. Just when I thought real love didn't exist, he showed me it did!

THE UNVEILING

CHAPTER 15

THE NEXT CHAPTER

(And It All Begins)

Sometimes you get to what you thought was the end and you find it's a whole new beginning.
—Anne Tyler

I didn't know how to love without fear, but I was willing to take a chance to believe in him and give us a shot. I had given up on love, not believing it existed. However, he proved me wrong. The kind of love I had in my life previously was toxic and unhealthy. The men who said they loved me kept hurting me over and over again. Therefore, I was afraid to be loved because it came with suffering, and I was not sure if I could handle my heart being broken again. This man really loved me, and I believed he was going to end the cycle of pain and hurt in my life. *Please do not let me be wrong!*

After his almost near-death experience, he was starting to get stronger, and his jaw was no longer wired shut. I was falling more deeply in love with him as he fought through his most difficult and challenging moments. I overlooked all of his physical imperfections and accepted what I believed to be his genuine heart. He got a job, which increased his self-esteem. He never felt good enough to be with me, but I appreciated what he did to make me happy in the ways he could. He saw himself as more of a man once he started working and was able to take me out on dates and buy me gifts. We had been dating for about six or seven months and I did not want to think the worst, but it was difficult to not expect to be let down. I thought pain was all I deserved… I had to convinced myself otherwise. The first time he said, "I love you," I paused in the moment before repeating those same three words. I believed I loved him in the same way that he did me, although I was afraid to tell him. Saying, "I Love You," was rolling off our lips at the end of every conversation after that.

What made me even more intrigued is when he came along with me to visit my mother's grave on Mother's Day, it was the first time since she'd passed away that I'd been there. Which was almost four years ago. I struggled with the idea of going but he convinced me to go and said he would be by my side and he was. He held me in his arms and comforted me as I cried like a baby and that was a defining moment for me. That moved him up on the love chart a little more; he was winning me over rather quickly.

We started attending church and his family loved us together and so did I, we were a real couple. Taking the kids out and spending time with them was just as important as our alone time together. I loved his girls and they loved me back because I was a mother figure for them as their biological mom was not involved in their life. We spent time with one another's families, and we were getting closer, especially in our faith. My family still could not fully comprehend the nature of my relationship with him, but they accepted it because they loved me and wanted me to be happy and I was.

He was becoming more confident with working, gaining weight back, going to the gym, changing his wardrobe, and being able to purchase a used car. I was excited for him because I knew how much it meant to him to not only be a man but also feel like one who could contribute to our family. He appreciated how I stood by him through the worst parts of his life. I loved him and I did exactly what I was supposed to do, and that was to not give up on him during his most vulnerable times. He trusted me to be there for him and I didn't want to let him down.

I had become a different woman and for once was with a man who was the missing puzzle piece to my heart. We were approaching a year and he was still treating me like fine wine and a queen. He cooked me gourmet meals, and took me out on spontaneous dates. I finally felt worthy of love and deserved the way he was treating me. We were not perfect, but he was giving me the best kind of love and he seemed to enjoy loving me.

He Popped the Question

After a little more than a year, he asked me to marry him, and I said yes. What an awesome Christmas present! To finally find someone who loves me was what I needed. He made me feel safe to love him back. After staring at my ring for a while, it was time to share the news with both family and friends; certain members of my family, like my sister, were a little skeptical, but if I was happy that was all that mattered. Our children—especially his girls—were so happy. My three boys, well the two older ones, didn't care one way or the other, but if it was what I wanted then so be it. They were young, I do not think they understood the entire concept of a marriage, but I knew they liked him. My youngest boy accepted it right away, but he was still holding on to me reconciling with his father, although it had been years of us not being together.

This marriage was going to be different and better because God was the head and center of our lives. We went to church every Sunday and Bible study on Wednesdays. We both believed in each other and the sanctity of marriage. God was doing something different in me and I could not understand or explain it all, but I was seeing a change in my life and my family noticed it too. I was serving on a ministry at church and growing more spiritually in the Lord. I was excited to start my new life as his wife.

My sister wanted me to be happy, but she always felt he was not the man for me. She was protective of me! She continued to believe I was with him because I felt sorry that he almost lost his life. She didn't think I honestly loved him, but I did. She was only worried because she didn't want me getting hurt in any way, and I respected her concerns. She and I were always a team; we stuck together through everything, and I didn't want her to think that would change because I was marrying him. We were inseparable, nothing could tear us apart and I was not going to let it happen then!

My sister and I had discussed her moving into her own apartment. It seemed like more talk than desire because of how close we were. To our surprise, the apartment she had been waiting for became available much sooner than we had expected. We were both elated, yet anxious about her moving into her first apartment. She was an independent young lady, and I knew she would do fine on her own. We literally cried the day she moved, mostly because of separation anxiety. We had always been together. It was going to be tough for the both of us, but she only moved 10 minutes away. However, it probably worked out better that way because once I got married my husband and his daughters would move in with me.

With me working at night, it had been easy to work that shift without worrying about a babysitter. I began taking the kids to my sister's place on my way to work, which was becoming a headache, but they could not stay home alone. Those were the times that I missed my sister living with me. When my fiancé would stay over, the children could sleep in their own beds. I loved my job, but I was not sure how much longer I would be able to work that shift. Putting the needs of my children ahead of my own was priority but looking for a new job making the same money would be challenging. It was a tough decision, but I had to look for another job. Although it was difficult to leave a careered job that I had been at for four years, my children were first in my life.

I started the search for a new job and within a couple of weeks I got an offer; not my ideal job because it was a $5 an hour pay cut. God knows I didn't want to accept that, but the hours were what I needed, and the prison had no idea when or if I could change to day shift. I gave my two weeks' notice then started my new job. My income changed drastically, but I had better control of my schedule and my sleep… it was ideal for my family.

Blindsided

This gave me more time to spend with my fiancé, but for some reason he started to change. I did not want to think too much of it, but I was not going to ignore it and not talk about it. I mentioned to him that I noticed he was going out more often on the weekends than usual. I saw nothing wrong with having a discussion about it, but it caused an unnecessary argument. He was acting strange and somewhat arrogant, and that's when I became suspicious. *Why would he get so upset, I only made a comment about him hanging out?* I regretted saying something, upsetting him was the last thing I wanted to do. I didn't want to believe he was cheating; I thought we were in a great place. Old habits are hard to break!

I started looking through his cellphone and finding inappropriate text messages from other women. I wanted to convince myself it wasn't true because that was better than believing it was. I had given this man my heart, something that was not easy to do, only to find out he was being unfaithful. I couldn't believe he would do something like that to me—*Why would he?* I was confused and my heart was broken because I believed in him and us.

I confronted him and we had another argument, this time it was worse than before and he said things to me I didn't think he was capable of. I saw a side of him I did not know was there. I asked him to leave my house because we obviously needed a break from each other. I was in tears, so upset as I called my sister to tell her what had happened. Let's just say she was not too pleased and hoped I didn't go back to him. *How did we get here?* I invested so much of my time and trust into our relationship. I didn't want to throw it all away, just yet!

He made it seem like it was my fault for looking through his phone;

this was not the man I fell in love with. We were planning to get married to live a forever life together; I trusted him to take care of my heart and not damage it more than it had already been. *How could he betray me like this and treat me like I did not mean anything to him?* I literally could not gather the thought of how this man went from being loving, gentle, and kind to heartless and disrespectful. Loving him was easy until he became unlovable. It was a bit disappointing, yet I still wanted him. I was not sure if putting myself out there again was the best decision to make, however, it seemed like the right thing to do.

He was staying with his mother at the time, so one evening, I decided to go over there unannounced with the kids to see where we stood as a couple—that was not a good idea. I learned he was still being unfaithful, and it turned into a physical altercation. He actually put his hands on me, hitting me in my face. I knew I had to get away from him as I looked over and saw my sons in the doorway while he had me on the floor standing over me with a balled-up fist ready to strike again. Seeing their mother be abused is something I never wanted my sons to witness. He moved from over me and told me to leave. I stood up from the floor and I grabbed my children, left his mother's house, and drove all the way home in tears. I thought he was different from the others he proved to be the same. I wondered what my children were thinking; I was too ashamed to ask.

Breaking off the engagement was a no-brainer, but I was not okay with the decision. I had to face my family, especially my sister who never trusted him from the beginning. Although they were disappointed, they still supported whatever future decision I would make. My sister had animosity toward him for physically hurting me and she did not want to forgive him. *Maybe it was me that made him react that way*. I was struggling with what had happened.

After all I had been dealing with in my past relationships, I finally trusted someone to love me, now this. I was discouraged. My self-esteem had taken a huge hit, leaving me feeling defeated. *What about me wasn't good enough?* It seemed like everyone I loved was hurting or leaving me.

It wasn't long before I started thinking about the good times we had in our relationship and regretting our separation. I made every attempt to move on from my past, and I thought he was the one to move forward with. Turns out, I had fallen in love with the wrong man… again! Those feelings made me question and not trust myself with love.

About a month after the breakup, the phone calls were becoming more frequent, the apologies were never-ending, and "please forgive me, I will do anything to get you back" was pulling on my heartstrings. I was missing him and maybe he made a mistake and giving him another chance couldn't be that bad, could it? I had become much more forgiving due to my walk with the Lord. My relationship with Him (God) was growing and getting stronger; he deserved to be forgiven and so I did.

When I told my family that he was back in my life, no one was happy about it; my sister especially was not thrilled about it. Others asked, "Are you sure?"

No, I was not at all sure, but it was worth the risk. My children didn't feel the same about him and it was difficult having him around them.

My sons never forgot what they saw and their feelings for him had changed; they were not at the slightest pleased about us reconciling, but they felt they had no choice in the matter. I did not expect them to forget, but I wanted us all to get along again as best we could.

The wedding was back on, and it was six months away, and we decided we would only go on dates and not have sexual intimacy until our wedding night. Well, our pastor advised it—boy, were we in for the challenge of our lives.

Marriage counseling with our pastor was a must. She believed in us and wanted the best for us, although at one point she had her doubts. She thought my fiancé was not mature enough to handle the responsibilities of being a husband, and under no circumstances did she agree with him hitting me. I loved him so much and wanted nothing but to be his wife, I somehow had to trust him again. There were times it was hard to think about the pain he caused me. But I knew I had to get past the betrayal if we were going to make it down the aisle.

As we started over, we actually were getting along better like in the beginning of our relationship. Trusting that he would love me right and respect me made becoming his wife less of a challenge.

We were moving along with our wedding plans and the excitement of it all felt right. I mean, we had a few disagreements in between but nothing too devastating not to move forward with the wedding. It was really happening; I couldn't believe it! After all we had been through, we were still going to be joined together as husband and wife.

The morning of had come and I was nervous, my stomach had butterflies, and I was eager to meet my soon-to-be husband to become one in front of family and friends. It was time to meet him at the altar and as I gathered myself to walk down the aisle, I hoped that I was being placed in good hands. I didn't want to entertain any negative thoughts about me making a mistake; he was the one and I was convinced. Our vows were from the heart, the tears covered our faces, and we were joined as husband and wife. I had married the man I would commit the rest of my life and love to at all times. "For better, for worst, for richer, for poorer, in sickness, and in health."

Blended Family

The honeymoon was over, and we were back home to where the seven of us would be under one roof. My three boys and his two girls were now our five children. While I knew it was not going to be easy, I wanted it to work and so it began. We all settled into the house and had a family meeting to see how everyone was feeling about the change. We shared our expectations as a family together and individually. Trust is what we wanted everyone to have along with love. We did not expect magic to happen overnight, but we wanted to function as a loving and supportive family. It was summertime, so the kids had time to get to know one another more before school started back in the fall. We spent our days and nights adjusting to living in the same house. No matter how difficult things were, I wanted us to develop a close bond as a blended family.

I realized it wasn't as simple for the girls as I thought it would be, especially his older daughter who was eight at the time. I guess you never truly know someone until you live with him or her. I assumed the girls liked me because I adored them, but somehow after a few weeks I noticed a change in their behavior. It became more like a competition between the girls and me for the attention of their dad. I think they had difficulties sharing his time with me. I had talks with my husband about what I noticed, and he didn't believe it to be true. He thought I was overreacting. Going to work started to feel like a getaway for me, and it was too soon to have those feelings. The girls were used to being raised by my husband and his mom, their grandmother. Maybe the expectations of what I wanted were too high and I was not taking into consideration it was brand new to them. I was trying to make the transition with the girl's smooth and set clear boundaries at the same time. In my house there were a set of rules to follow. That didn't mean my sons were perfect, they were far from it, but they were familiar with discipline—something the girls had a difficult time adjusting to.

A couple of months into the marriage, my husband and I were already having disagreements over the girls. I wanted to teach them with limitations, and he thought I was being too hard and enforcing too many rules. Maybe I should have slowed down, giving myself more time to bond and establish trust. His oldest daughter was becoming rebellious and difficult to manage, and I wasn't as equipped to deal with that as I thought. I had all boys and raising girls was different, and honestly, I didn't know what to do. She started to become disrespectful toward me and disruptive in the home. The boys were no longer happy, and the blended household was not blending well at all. I grew bitter because my husband seemed to not understand and would blame me for the rift, saying I was the adult and should know how to handle the girls.

Everyone seemed to be going in different directions and our home was in disarray. My husband and I couldn't agree on anything when it came to the girls and the older daughter knew we were not on the same page and played us against each other. The younger daughter was pulled into going along with her sister's shenanigans. It had become a nightmare for me—it was unbelievable, so I wanted to return those girls back to their grandmother. I was failing at trying to make it work. I started to have unpleasant feelings toward them and no longer wanted them in my space. *How could this be? Could I turn it around?* My marriage was in jeopardy after just a few months. When you want it to work you must go to great lengths to do it.

I was the adult; I should've known better. It was my responsibility to fix it and get my house in order. There was no way I was going to allow an 8-year-old little girl to dictate how life was going to be for me in my own home. I suggested to my husband that we all have a talk to get a better understanding of the tension between everyone. I never wanted it to be like that; I thought we would all get along and be one big happy family, and the opposite happened.

During our talk, everyone seemed to struggle with expressing how they were feeling. Well, except for me. And little Miss Thing made sure she said it seemed like I didn't like her. Being the adult, I had to acknowledge what she said, asking her to explain herself. Once she did, we came to an understanding that we both would try our best to make our relationship work. I loved those girls. I was their mother and they needed to trust me, especially since their biological mom had walked out on them. At the time, I didn't understand that was probably why she struggled to let me in completely; she didn't trust me to stay. Or, maybe she felt like I took her place with her dad. Whatever it was, I didn't want to make her feel like I was taking her father away from her.

Although there continued to be issues, things started to get a little better between the girls and I, but then the boys came to me saying they no longer wanted them to stay with us. They said the girls were annoying and they didn't want them as sisters—*what was I supposed to do with that?* We were going from one extreme to the next, trying to figure out the best way to build and strengthen a healthy family unit. I was hoping that once school started that things would get better; they would not be around each other all day.

Blended family problems were challenging to manage, especially because I seemed to be in it alone most of the time. We needed to work together as a team, yet it seemed more like we had become separate families within our household. My husband continued getting along with the boys, while the girls and I were still working to establish better communication. I knew it would not be an overnight process, but the reality was it could take more time than I wanted to admit.

THE UNVEILING

CHAPTER 16

THE ROLLER COASTER RIDE

(Up and Down)

With peaks of joy and valleys of heartache, life is a roller coaster ride that's both scary and exciting at the same time-the rise and fall of which defines our journey.
—SebastiAn

My husband and I were definitely drifting away in our communication about the girls, at times I did not want to talk, it only led to more disagreements. He was experiencing the tension in the home as well and tried to stay out of it rather than correct the girls. He did not want to feel like he was choosing sides but if you ask me, he did choose.

He would spend time with the boys and I with the girls and then we all came together for movie night, church, dinner, and other family outings. It wasn't easy but we were doing our best to make it work. I was hoping we would all get along and be on the same page so we could live our lives as a blended family. It had been several months since they moved in, I was going at a fast pace, everyone was different in their own way, maybe I needed to slow it down. Of course, I wanted us to merge as a family overnight and immediately adjust to the changes.

As time went on, I started to see light at the end of the tunnel with the children. They were actually getting along. The girls loved their new school, and the boys were starting to see them as their sisters. We laughed a little more and no matter how things were before it was getting a little smoother—until the unthinkable happened.

The Deception

I just knew I had to be wrong; at least I wanted to be. Those familiar feelings of my husband being dishonest started to surface again. *Was it my insecurities?* Yes, we had some disagreements and heated arguments but none of that should've called for him to want to cheat. My suspicion was growing at a rapid pace, and I started to snoop. I hated that I was put in that situation again. Our children were finally getting along as siblings, not perfectly but definitely better, and the girls and I were in a good space. *Why would he jeopardize that progress?*

Well, my feelings were absolutely accurate: I found a number with a woman's name on it. *What do I do with it?* I called, of course, hoping it was a relative I didn't know, but no, it was someone he had met. After a lengthy conversation with her she told me that nothing sexual happened between them, not because of him but because she didn't allow it to happen. They had been talking and he'd bring her lunch on her job and they went out on a date once. She was not aware that he was married, and I believed her. I was at a loss for words, but I thanked her for being honest and she assured me that she would not be seeing him again. Whether I believed her or not was irrelevant; I needed to deal with my husband.

I confronted him, and as usual he turned it around on me. He said all I did was nag him and that's why he does not like being home. I couldn't believe he would do this to me again; I trusted him to love me and never hurt me again as he said he wouldn't. I was so used to fixing all of the problems that I was already thinking in my head how to do better so he wouldn't cheat. *Why did I make it my fault and responsibility? In my head,* it had to have been something I did wrong; otherwise, why would he cheat? He was right, I nagged him too much and no man wants to deal with that. I needed to change my ways because I was forcing him into the arms of other women!

The next day, I just needed to know why… there I go nagging again. I told him how hurt I was about what he'd done, and he had to promise not to do it again. I thought back to when he was a kind and gentle man, and I could talk to him about any and everything. He definitely was not the same man. *What happened to him?* Instead of him addressing my feelings he blew up at me as if I had no right to question him. The children were home, and I didn't want to have that type of conversation with him in front of or around the children; I knew it would get out of control and it did. The argument got worst, and this man was about to hock spit in my face because he couldn't handle hearing the truth, or as he would call it *nagging*. I grabbed a knife and I dared him to spit on me and he looked me dead in my face saying, "You are not worth my spit."

He called me all types of horrible names. He degraded me as a woman, calling me fat and telling me nobody would want me. I was humiliated; he knew how I felt about my weight, and he used it to further hurt me. This was a bad dream that turned into a nightmare.

I called my sister crying telling her what happened, so she came to my house. When she arrived, the disgust on her face needed no words and she said to him, "I wish you would have spit on my sister."

She was tougher than I was. I had grown weak and vulnerable for this man. She told me to grab some clothes and the boys and to come stay with her for a couple of days. She wanted to get me away from that toxic situation. I left with her, but I was devastated. He was my husband; *how could he treat me like this?* That incident further caused her to not like him. I didn't know what I was going to do about my marriage. He really was going to spit in my face!

I later learned that he called our pastor telling her that I had left the home but coincidentally left out the reasons why, completely blaming me. My pastor called me saying my husband told her I was no longer at the home. I admired and trusted my pastor, so I took what she was saying into consideration and after our conversation I had time to think. After two days, I went back home to fix our marriage. He apologized to me for everything he said, saying he did not mean any of it. I wanted to believe him, but I struggled with his words in my head. He suggested we have a counselor meeting with our pastor, and I agreed. I was willing to do whatever was necessary to make our marriage work. I did not want to give up so quickly.

She was able to meet with us right after Sunday service, I was still mad but open to getting some help. Just when I thought my husband could not stoop any lower. The church we belonged to was big on making the men feel in charge of the women, while the women are submissive in every way. He made himself out to be a victim and I was the villain. He pulled the nagging card, and it went downhill from there. The one thing we would hear at church was, "Don't no man want no nagging women," followed by scripture to back it up. Proverbs 21:9, "Better to live on a corner of the roof than share a house with a quarrelsome wife."

It was the worst meeting and I felt like my husband ambushed me and I was defenseless. The pastor and her husband tried to get me to listen as they attempted to reconcile the situation between us, but I completely shut down. I just wanted to escape. I was in tears as they were all trying to get me to reason and understand; I just wasn't in the right mindset to do so. Feelings of defeat overwhelmed me! Was anyone going to address the spitting and cheating situation? Or should I assume nagging was worst?

Our drive home was intense and quiet, and my heart was just as broken as I was. Life as I knew it with him was never the same after that, although we remained a family. The trust was destroyed, and he continued to lie and cheat. I found myself on the phone with other women whose numbers I found more than I could have ever imagined. The arguing and disagreements became a part of our daily routine. I was becoming paralyzed and stuck, not knowing what to do next. I didn't know how to walk away from my family, although I knew this wouldn't end well. He was physically wearing me out and I wanted to keep pretending like nothing was wrong while he chipped away at my heart.

Our one-year anniversary had arrived and celebrating seemed far from right. He had put me through so much, especially the past few months while our blended family was trying to bond, he was sneaking behind my back with other women.

My sister told me he was not the one for me, but I wanted to go through with the wedding anyways and then my marriage was falling apart. I was beat up mentally, spiritually, and emotionally. He appeared to be the best man for me, yet he was ripping me to shreds and I was sick about it. *How could I constantly allow him to treat me that way?* Moving on from the situation is what I should have done before I said, "I Do."

Despite the darkness in my soul, I had the audacity to still celebrate our one-year anniversary. It was on a Sunday after church and his mother kept the children while we spent the evening together. We had a lovely dinner, laughed, took pictures like a happily married couple, and walked around the lake. He had a way with me, touching my soft spots and knowing I would love him through it all and so I did! We made it through without arguing and without me bringing up his transgressions and infidelity.

I attempted to fix my marriage because I didn't want to be divorced for the second time and I loved this man—as shameful as I felt for loving him, I still did. I felt stupid staying in a marriage with a man who clearly didn't want me, which is why I kept telling myself I deserved better. I just wasn't sure how to get it. What example was I setting for my children? They could see I was no longer happy no matter how hard I tried to hide it.

The children could feel the tension between us, but I did my best to make home comfortable and peaceful. It was so challenging. I cried more than I laughed, and he continued to expect to have sex with me. I never refused him because I believed in what I was being taught—that when you are married your body is no longer yours; it belongs to your husband. I would lie on my back many nights wanting it to be over after he had cursed me out earlier in the day. I felt like a piece of cheap, slaughtered meat rather than a wife. I was becoming overwhelmingly sad and the weight of my marriage and raising five children was getting the best of me. I was losing the battle and just wanted to feel safe again. I was in a sunken place and becoming emotionally reckless!

One day, I had to go pay a ticket at the courthouse (15 minutes away) and got lost on my way there. I drove around for more than three hours trying to find my way back in an area I was quite familiar with. I was having a nervous breakdown and didn't know it. Why else would I get lost going to a place I'd been several times before? I hated home and what had become of my life. I had to get it together because the children needed me, and I had to be a mother no matter what I was going through.

At this point I was settling trying to hold on to Godly principles and my pastor's word. Always being afraid to ask my husband questions or to have a discussion about important matters because I did not want to seem like a nag. Here we go again. The bills were due that he needed to pay. You would have thought I asked him to jump off the Empire State Building. The argument led to us almost getting into a physical fight, but he left as he usually did to avoid answering to me. I waited to give him time to cool off, hoping he would come back home, but he did not. This was only 2 ½ months after our one-year anniversary, *I guess we won't be celebrating a second one.*

Double-Crossed

After a few hours, I called him, but he didn't answer. I continued to attempt to reach him by phone—no response. Called his mom and she hadn't seen or heard from him. I was worried and hoped nothing had happened to him. My husband did not come home until the next morning. I was furious; he walked in with no explanation as if I didn't deserve one and went to lie down in the bed. I was unsure how to handle the situation without sounding like a nag, but I had every right to be angry. While he was in bed, I asked him where he had been, but he didn't answer. He told me to leave him alone and stop asking him questions. I was his wife, I deserved answers. Of course, in my mind he had been out all night with another woman—it wouldn't be the first time.

All my rage surfaced, and I couldn't take it anymore. I asked him to leave, or I would call the police. He ignored me, which infuriated me even more, so I called the police to have him removed. That made him so angry, but the police said they couldn't make him leave but did advise him to take a walk until things calmed down. I was glad the kids were in school and didn't have to witness another unfortunate dispute between us. I felt so bad about what I had done involving the police, but I was so tired of the way he continued to disrespect me and not treat me like his wife. He didn't answer when I tried to call and apologize, but why did I feel the need to say sorry? I was afraid I had gone too far, and he was going to leave me!

Several hours later, my husband returned home with a U-Haul truck and his cousin to help him move all of his and the girls' things out of the house. I could not believe it was happening, I blamed myself; it was my fault that he was leaving and saying that I shouldn't have called the police. I held back my tears and pain but deep inside I wanted to beg him to stay and ask how I could make it better, but the words wouldn't come out of my mouth. After he loaded the last thing on the truck, he said he was going to withdraw the girls from school, and they were never coming back… and neither was he. My husband walked out on me and our marriage. I was stunned! Life for me had abruptly shifted right before my eyes.

I called his mother telling her what happened. I begged her to not allow him back in her house, to send him back home to me, his wife, where he belonged. I felt abandoned, I wanted to be loved so badly that I was willing to stay in a toxic marriage with a man who did not love or value me. *Who had I become to allow myself to be treated so unfairly? Why did I accept this for so long and willing to do it again?*

Once the boys arrived at home from school they said, "Mommy, we didn't see the girls."

The children always walked home together. I explained to them what happened in a way they could understand without telling them too much, and surprisingly they were not upset. They said, "We are glad they are gone because nothing has been the same."

I wasn't sure how to respond in that moment. I needed time to myself to process all that happened so quickly.

The Breakdown

As the morning neared, I was sick to my stomach, hoping it was all a dream... but it wasn't. He wasn't there next to me. I looked around the room and all of his stuff was gone. I was at a loss over what had happened. My sister felt bad for me because I was hurting, but she was not at all upset that he was gone and hoping he didn't come back. She kept telling me, "I will be here for you," and she was when I allowed her to.

She knew the emotional and mental abuse I endured, and she hated him for it. He really left me—walked out of our marriage like it was never real for him and maybe it was not. That explains how it was so easy for him to be unfaithful—he never took our vows serious.

The girls were calling me every day crying asking to come home and I did not know what to say to help comfort them. I was hoping this would only be temporary and they would come back home soon. I felt like a failure, my purpose for life was dwindling down to nothing. I was struggling and fighting not to fall completely apart. I wanted my husband back so bad. Why would I want someone who treated me like that? But I missed him so much. It had only been a few days, but it felt like years, before I was feeling like I should fight to win him back. It was easier to stay with what I was familiar with than to start over, I wanted another chance to make it right.

One evening, he called. I was hoping it was to say he was coming home, but he didn't know what to say beyond his usual, "I'm sorry." I accepted his apology, but I wanted more from him. I wanted him to be a husband, father, and the man I fell in love with—all of which he didn't want to do. After we ended our conversation, I pondered on the words, "I love you." Within a week or so of him being gone he was seeing another woman, which further deepened the wounds he had caused that I wasn't sure I would be able to heal. *Where did she come from? How could he be committed to someone else so soon?* I lost focus and was consumed with him being with another woman. Even with him gone, this man was still breaking me down, and I was allowing him to do it. I went to work and then straight home to my room every day, shutting everybody out of my life. I didn't want to be bothered. My children were noticing I was becoming different and distant from them. I barely cooked meals, but they ate what was quick and easy. I didn't have the energy to do a lot.

Why did I take this man back only for him to do me like this, was a constant thought in my mind. I guess the abused little girl in me was never emotionally healed, and I was still looking to fill the emptiness of my unhealed wounds. My heart was so sad all of the time it was an indescribable ache. Just to breathe was becoming a task. Work was overwhelming; I was taking bathroom breaks to cry. The expectations of home were demanding, and I couldn't keep up. Church was emotional; seeing his family and the girls was depressing. I was pitiful.

I didn't want to move on without him so when he would call asking to see me, mostly late at night, I wasn't strong enough to say no.

He knew I was emotionally weak for him. Therefore, I made myself available to have sex with him, knowing he had moved on with another woman. But he was still my husband. I found out through the girls the girlfriend had moved in with him at his mother's house after one month of him moving out of our house.

I could not lose him to her, so I decided to fight for him, and I'm sure he enjoyed watching the show. He manipulated and deceived me for months as he played on my emotional vulnerability. I became his side chick, the one he was cheating with and not on. My self-esteem was depleted, and my self-worth had become rotten to the core. I had become emotionally unavailable to my children because my only interest was getting my husband back. I was struggling with my state of being. At the same time, I watched as he played me like a fool, and he knew I was craving his love and affection. I knew this man was not right me, but I wanted to love him anyway. He was so disrespectful to me, and I was holding on to the good parts of who he used to be.

One afternoon, he came to spend the day with me, and when it was time for him to leave, I asked if he could stay a little longer and he became upset. He said, "This is why I shouldn't be with you, you're ungrateful and should appreciate the time I am giving you. You know I have to go back home to her."

I apologized for not appreciating the time he gave me, asking him not to be mad at me. I didn't want to risk him not coming back, so I just went along with the way he wanted things to be. Every time he left me to go back to her, my soul crushed more. I wanted to believe his words that he was coming back home but needed more time to work on him; yes, I believed him. I was a fool!

We had plans to go to dinner. He was picking me up from work, so I told my ride that I was okay because my husband was coming to get me. My car was in the shop, so I had a coworker giving me rides for the week. It was pouring down raining, and I waited, looking out the window at each drop of rain. I called him what seemed like a thousand times; he never answered. After about an hour I knew he wasn't coming, all I could do was cry. There I was being thrown a curve ball, waiting and he never showed up—another blow to my heart. I was ready to give up on life; I couldn't take it anymore. My mind had been poisoned by his manipulation. I was thankful that my cousin was able to pick me up, otherwise I would have been stranded. Riding in her car was sobering because once again I fell for his deception and lies. *Was I ever going to get enough of this?*

Two nights later, he called apologizing saying he forgot, and I accepted it again. I tried to be an understanding wife, but I told him he couldn't keep treating me like that. He came over to see me that night, spewing out more lies that I unfortunately wanted to believe. He was using the love he knew I had for him to his advantage, but I was too weak, and my spirit was too broken to fight. I was so embarrassed about the woman I allowed myself to become for him. I was in competition with another woman to win back my husband. *How foolish was I?* I was hanging on to him no matter how much my heart was breaking.

One early morning a little after 5am, my phone rang, and it was him crying, begging, and pleading, asking if he could come get me so we could go to the morning prayer at our church that started at 6am. He hadn't been to church for months, but it was what I prayed for. So, when he called I was moved by his request to go to Morning Prayer thinking this would change things. I agreed and allowed him to pick me up, believing the Lord had answered my prayers. Afterward he took me to breakfast, and we talked about everything. He told me the other woman was pregnant, but she lost the baby. He said he was tired and knew he had made a lot of mistakes and was ready to come back home. He said he was no longer seeing the other woman. Was it even normal for me to still want to fix my marriage after all he had done? I was willing to give it a try. I did not want to show too much excitement, but I asked him if he was sure he wanted to come back home and he said, "Yes, I love you and miss my family."

He said he would be home later that evening once he packed him and the girl's things. My face lit up like a Christmas tree, I was getting my family back! I couldn't wait for the end of the day as I was preparing for his return. I was anxious; it was time for him to come home. He'd been gone for nearly eight months!

I waited, going back and forth to the window every time I heard what sounded like a truck pulling up. I was like a little kid waiting for her long-lost daddy to show up. It was getting late, and I had not heard from him, I did not want to sound pushy, but he said he was coming home. I called him and he answered the phone like I was bothering him, and we didn't have a magical moment earlier in the day. I asked him what time I should expect him, and his response was, "I never told you I was coming today. See this is what I am talking about with you."

He said I was pressuring him again, and he would let me know when he is ready. Was I in the twilight zone? Because I was beginning to think I was crazy? This roller coaster ride was spinning me out of control. I hung up crying again. I questioned myself all over again: *Why did you fall for it?* I couldn't help that I loved someone who continued to shame me and break my heart. No matter what he did, I still wanted to be with him. My love for him did not go away because of the pain he caused, I wished it did. I was so tired of fighting to be loved by him, begging him to stay, and forcing myself on him.

The next morning, I woke up, got the kids out for school, and as clear as day the Lord told me to go over to my husband's house. Well, I didn't want to go because I wanted to be done with him and all of his lies. But I got dressed anyway, got in my car, and while driving down the road the Lord whispered in my ear, "It's going to hurt you, but you will be okay."

I didn't understand, and surely, I didn't need any more hurt from him. I arrived at his house and his mom and brother were sitting at the kitchen table. I asked where my husband was, and they said in the basement. As I was approaching the basement steps, I could hear him in the shower. Why is he up so early in the shower? He wasn't going to work because he did not have a job. When I got close to him, he looked shocked and the first thing he said was, "Don't go back there."

Well, "back there" was his bedroom, and of course I went anyway. I understood why he didn't want me back there: He had a woman in his bed, not even the one he was seeing from before. He hopped out of the shower so fast getting dressed, but at this time I had all the information I needed from her. I began fighting, pushing, and shoving him; I completely lost control of myself. Every curse word I could gather came out of my mouth; once again he treated me like the other woman, making it my entire fault for showing up unannounced. I almost allowed myself to believe if I didn't show up, I would not have seen him with the women. I was so used to taking the blame and apologizing for things he'd done wrong to me, and in that moment I almost did it again. I had to be done. He was not going to change; he was everything I didn't need. My love for him was the strongest feeling I had at that time. I wished I loved myself a little more than I loved him. Unfortunately, every setback felt worse than the one before.

As I walked back upstairs behind him and the woman, I wanted to kill them both. His mother and brother looked as if they didn't know the woman was downstairs. I do not believe they did, otherwise they would not have allowed me down there. She and my husband left, and his mother attempted to calm me down. I told her I was completely done with her son, and I was never coming back to her house. She tried to encourage me, saying I was just upset but we will get past it and get it together. There was nothing else left to get together!

I walked out of that front door and before I could open my car door, I broke down crying. I cried, screamed, and hollered all the way home. I was truly at an all-time low and I needed God to take care of me. I knew my husband did not deserve another ounce of me, he was not capable of love. Once I got home, I went to my bedroom and crawled in my bed praying to God to please help me! God had to do for me what I couldn't do for myself.

CHAPTER 17

HEALING FROM MY PAIN

(It Was Time)

Although the world is full of suffering, it is full also of the overcoming of it.
—Helen Keller

I was so lost and uncertain as to how and when I was going to lift my head up from the pillow. This man had done everything in his power to destroy me and break me down. I didn't have the mental or physical strength to think about what life would be like without him. I was bone-tired; for nearly a year my husband preyed on my feelings, emotions, and the love I had for him. I was his yo-yo and puppet, and he was stringing me along simply because he could. I had become trapped in the cat and mouse game he was playing. What I thought was love was not love at all.

Being that I was his wife, I assumed he would respect, honor, protect, and love me as he said he would. Instead, he dishonored and shattered me until I was in tiny, little fragile pieces. I felt like damaged goods that needed to be thrown away like trash. I couldn't pull myself up from the gutter; I had been there for so long. I got to a place in my life where I could not tell the difference between love and hate because they felt and looked the same at that point.

His words said that he loved me, but his actions proved otherwise.

I knew I had a toxic childhood and other bad relationships, but I was hoping for something different from him. What I had been through as a child is why I was having so many problems in life and relationships. I was going through my trauma alone and looking for ways for others to heal and fix what was damaged inside of me. I blamed myself for the actions of other people for so long that I carried that mentality throughout my adulthood. Always taking on the responsibility and feeling like I had to fix it. Furthermore, it was difficult to express my feelings because of the shame I felt behind the abuse.

I had become preoccupied with the thoughts of what my husband had been doing to me. I tried to put on a brave face so my children couldn't see how badly bruised my heart was. I knew going back to my husband was not an option and I needed the courage to stay away. He waited, as he often did, to call as if he was giving me time to process his betrayal. I wanted to fall prey to his baseless words as I always did, but I knew that time I couldn't. I had to move past him and the memories of the pain. Thinking of it was holding me back and keeping me from moving forward to freely living life. I wanted to get stronger. Prayer and meditation was helping, but I needed more... so I sought counseling.

My weekly appointments were refreshing. They gave me a chance to share my feelings with someone who wasn't biased. My counselor allowed me to freely speak, offering solutions, and I shared everything that was on my heart with him, but he would mostly say, "You already have the answers; just keep talking."

He even called me a breath of fresh air, getting nuggets of wisdom from me to use for other clients. It felt good to have positive reinforcement after so much negativity in my life.

What I had been through with my husband felt different from the other relationships. Perhaps it was how long I stayed and accepted the betrayal, mistrust, abuse, infidelity, and the list goes on. In truth, I held on because I was too afraid to let go. I asked myself many times why I found comfort in staying, no answer made sense, besides it was familiar and easier to stay than to leave. That marriage and he had a grip on me that was too tight to pull away from.

I wanted to feel love from my husband that he could no longer give me, and I do not think he loved himself. My life with him had changed in ways that had me detached from my emotions. I had been harboring resentment long before he ever came into the picture. As I already said, staying with him through the betrayal and infidelity only made me disconnect even more from reality.

My heart felt beyond repair. I had given so much of my energy to my marriage and a man who stopped deserving me. I loved him with everything, and he didn't love me back. At some point, he became incapable of doing that. I lost touch with myself thinking something was there that was not. I was hoping the man he used to be would come back.

I was so determined not to have another failed marriage and be a twice-divorced woman that I sacrificed my life, peace, and happiness to stay in a marriage with a man who had long given up on me and us. I was always trying to correct his mistakes so he would see me as the perfect angel I once was to him. I was holding on to want I wanted him to be rather than what he was, it helped validate staying in the marriage. I did not belong in his heart anymore, although he was still in mine. I prayed many nights for God to fix it!

I wanted to do whatever it took to stay married, but nothing worked. I still felt the pain, even knowing my marriage was over. I tried my best to be a great wife loving him with the same love God loved me with. I had lost my way with my husband and almost my life too. I wanted to give up on life and everything proved I should, but my children were who saved me.

Unconsciously, I spent my entire life running from myself and all of the pain, trauma, and suffering I endured. I felt the need for somebody to love me at all cost, but no one seemed to know how to do that. I had been functioning in unhealthy relationships as if it was normal. I did not know how to be in a healthy relationship with myself or others—I was never taught how to be.

I started being sexually abused at 7 years old and from there my life went into a downward spiral. Unbeknownst to me, I went on with life not always knowing I was hurting because of it. I was forced into brokenness as a child and every experience afterward was a result of the trauma. The times when I didn't understand what I was doing with my life were challenging and confusing because I did not know what to do to make it better.

Coming to Terms

I was a fatherless daughter, which I believed played a part in the dysfunctional relationships with men along with the sexual abuse because my father was not there to keep me safe. He was in and out of my life until he passed away at 56 years old in the summer of 2006 from a stroke. I was 34 years old and I felt robbed when he died; I still needed him to show me how I should be loved, which he had failed to show while he was alive. My father had his own struggles with drugs and alcohol and had to figure out life at 14 years old. I was devastated over the loss of my father and furious at the same time.

Now I would never know what it's like for a man to love me right were my thoughts, which made me extremely selfish in the moment of his death. I was used to seeing men come and go; it started with the first man who was supposed to stay in my life—my father, I was not ready to permanently lose him. My life had been tarnished for so long, partly because he was not consistently in it. Now I was left figuring out how to grieve and heal in my own way. As I looked back over every inch of my life, he missed so much of it and everything I had gone through were the effects of all my bad childhood experiences and his absence, which left lasting impressions on me that couldn't easily be forgotten. My father was gone and there was nothing I could do about it. I knew I had to get over it. I truly admired him and wished we had more living to do together, more time to connect, and more time to love.

I practically raised myself after the death of my grandmother. Although my mother was present in my life, she was absent for what I needed most of the time and that was protection. I had to learn life on my own and it was not easy figuring it all out. My mother did all she knew to do but it didn't change the emptiness of love I was left to fill on my own. Maybe my mother never had healthy relationships and that is why she struggled to provide that for me. Either way I was forced into adult responsibilities without the proper example from both of my parents.

Growing up for me was complicated; I had built walls up that I was unaware were there that deepened as I got older. I attached myself to men for the attention I failed to get from my father, made all of the wrong choices and looked for love in all the places I should not have been. I did not realize how deep my wounds were and how much healing I needed from the damage that had been caused over the years. I had struggled with so much that I was not dealing with that I became mentally drained after learning how much of the pain in my life went unnoticed. I believed that was just the way I was, so I never addressed or changed it.

The hate I had inside of me from pretending to be alright, had emotionally damaged me. But I was never to blame and I had to stop condemning myself for everything that went wrong in my life that others had caused. The pent-up anger in me from being hurt in my marriages, violated as a child, and feeling shamed, caused me deeper pain and sorrow. Although I wanted to get revenge, it was time to let it all go. Facing the abuse, pain, and trauma was hard it was easier to act as if it never happened. Why was I responsible for mending what others had broken in me? But I was responsible and it was up to me to forgive those who hurt me. My questions

233

were—How do I start and where do I begin the process of healing this deep cycle of pain?

I Trusted The Process

I knew the healing process would be a lifetime; I had emotional wounds and painful scars that were cut too deep to heal overnight. I was done with lying and acting, as if I was okay when I was not. If you have never been hurt, then you will never understand pain. I understood pain in ways I never wanted to admit. It was too devastating to accept the truth, so I lied and covered up most of my suffering. I was tired of figuring out how to live life and acting strong when I was weak.

I had to stop having pity parties for my failed marriage. It wasn't my fault that he fell out of love with me and that he decided to choose another path and not commit to our vows. I did my best being his wife, support, and friend as he rejected all of my efforts to save our marriage. It had me paralyzed feeling so undeserving of the least respect. That was one of the major parts of my healing, knowing I had given my all in my marriage without any regrets. I only questioned why I stayed so long at times, until that question no longer mattered either.

I couldn't look back; I had to keep moving forward, toward a life without him in it. I had been standing in my own way, afraid of what was ahead. I wish I could erase all of the horrible things of my past, all of the mistreatment I endured from my husband, and start over without those memories… but that was impossible. Therefore, each day I was intentional about healing and mending the broken pieces of my heart.

I was fighting by the minute and the day to maintain, it was hard trying to overcome the feelings of helplessness. I was learning how to love myself and work through my problems. I was beyond heartbroken, I was mentally broken and I was not going to keep living there over and over again. I had become my own worst enemy over the years and I had the ability to turn things around. I had mistakenly believed I could never recover from my emotional and psychological traumas and enjoy life, but that was another lie I told myself. Instead, I would get stronger because of the rough upbringing and all the constant setbacks in my life.

The course of my healing was up and down, yet I was insistent on getting to that place of rebuilding and restoring my life. Healing takes time, it's a lifelong journey and I felt a lot of pain along the way, but it was necessary in order for me to push forward. Many times, I was ready to turn back, becoming tired, but I thanked God for carrying me every step of the way after being stuck in the betrayal of my marriage and waiting for my husband's approval to release me from his web of lies. When it was over I did not know how bound I was until I was no longer captive. Finally, I was free and would be better because of it, ready to face what was ahead of me and move on. Although, my future was unpredictable I was ready to go through the rest of the process in order to come out on the other side of my emotional pain!

Me and my handsome father, I loved him no matter what.

My father holding my youngest son at 2 weeks old 1992.

CHAPTER 18

I SURVIVED

(Everyone's Survival Story Is Different)

"My mission in life is not merely to survive, but to thrive; and to do so with some passion, some compassion, some humor, and some style."
—*Maya Angelou*

I was faced with many harrowing life changing trauma's and I had no way of knowing if or how I could bounce back and survive. My life had its uphill battles and valley lows, I was uncertain if my story would end well, but somehow, I emerged and managed to pull through with strength I didn't know I had. There was no changing anything that had happened to me and I could not continue to keep letting it make me worse. I found it extremely difficult to get out of the entrapment of abuse, pain, and trauma until I did.

All of the abuse I endured affected my life in one way or another. I had suffered through bad relationships, defeat, guilt, shame, sexual abuse, mental abuse, physical abuse, emotional abuse, molestation, trauma, divorce, single parenting, teenage pregnancy, dropping out of high school, rejection, loosing parents, loneliness, depression, suicidal thoughts, and the silencing of my voice.

Although it felt seemingly impossible to rise above my adversities and stand firm on what appeared to be a losing battle, I pulled myself up by my bootstraps and remained strong. Surely, I had all the reasons to lie down and die. However, I chose not to find myself in those same places or go down that same path of destruction as I did so many times. I was ready to face the emotional trauma's that happened to me and caused me so much pain as a child and as an adult. There was no denying the terrible things I had experience, most I didn't understand, but I survived trauma and that was a defining moment in my life.

> *"If you survived the trauma you will survive the recovery."*
> — Sara Paules.

I had struggled on how to manage adulthood because others had mismanaged my childhood and trust. Admitting the truth about abuse and trauma is never easy. I knew I had to allow myself that chance to experience the freedom of no longer being controlled by life's defeat and to put an end to the life I once knew. A vast majority of my life as a traumatized child and woman was spent in fear and pretending to be okay. I often wanted to forget about all the things that happened to me growing up, let alone talk about it. I knew it was possible to move forward and stop allowing the trauma to hold me back. All of the tears, nightmares, crying, anger, unanswered questions, feelings of isolation, betrayal, and bitterness I was left with, had to be managed and could no longer rule my life. Let me not make any mistakes here, I had triggers from my traumatic experiences, however, coming out of that dark place and no longer being emotionally disconnected from reality changed *how I survived.*

I wanted to live a life with purpose, a life that had meaning with an opportunity to live better than before. It was not enough for me to just survive my difficult circumstances, I wanted to learn how to thrive in a healthy and more fulfilling life. Things were still lingering, and I was trying hard not to ponder on my struggling thoughts, which tried to keep me hostage to the hurt. I told myself over and over again that I survived. And that meant more than the trauma itself. I was not in denial nor was I downplaying it, but I did not want to keep giving the trauma power. I'm blessed to have survived. There were more times than not when I was tired of fighting and trying, tired of holding on and praying, tired of expecting and waiting and nothing happening. But I didn't quit, although I had been knocked down many times with no desire to get back up.

Some days were easier to push through than others, but I had to do it there was no other choices for me. Being determined to keep my head above water took courage and boldness something I thought was lost a long time ago during my many emotional struggles. The constant reminders of my trauma were undeniable, but I went from a hopeless life to a hopeful life. And as a woman who have been a victim of trauma, loosing hope is inevitable. Trauma is tough and it can cause hate, envy, and bitterness, which can have a tight grip making it difficult to bounce back. But in the end of it, we have to choose which feelings we want to guide us through the rest of our lives, and I chose forgiveness of self and others.

There were many victories to celebrate. I did not get swallowed up in all of that mess, as I should have. I survived... and still I'm surviving. I am not a victim, but I' am a survivor of my trauma. I have endured some of the worst things in life and it is an ongoing process of getting to know who am after the trauma. It was hard to grapple with the thoughts of such a tumultuous past and to believe I had made it through all of it. When what should have killed you does not, your appreciation for life is beyond surviving the tragedy, it's living through it.

"Whatever horrible or hurtful things you have been through in your life, you have survived. You have endured. You have persevered. And that is why you should think of yourself as a trauma survivor, and not a trauma victim. Surviving trauma takes strength, resilience, and tapping into the miraculous, wonderful healing inner resources we all possess."

—Dan Roberts

With that said, I remember wanting to end it all as the weight of the hurt and damage it caused was overwhelming. It is easy to say what you would do until you have to do it and all of sudden those bright ideas are thrown out of the window. Some of us don't want to feel the pain, it hurts too bad and when it becomes a matter of life or death, you feel foolish for not knowing what to choose. There was no reason for me to justify or give validity to the trauma, it was just as wrong then as it is now. But surviving had been a turning point for me and I was ready to live in the present moment of my today and not in the past of my darkest yesterdays. Yes, I still struggled with loving myself, but I was still alive after it all and ready to get a jump start on happiness, life, and love.

The Upside of Trauma

You might think, after all I went through just to survive that I might be harboring hate towards those who hurt me, but it's just the opposite. Oh, trust me I did for a long time and wanted every person to pay for the damage that had been caused. I saw all of the people in my mind, along with everything they did to me, it would haunt me and I stayed alone with my thoughts every day. Being robbed of something changes you deeply on the inside, because it was taken from you without permission. Metaphorically speaking, the idea of not knowing if you will survive when someone rob you causes panic and vulnerability and your life flashes before your eyes.

I experienced a lot of final moments surrendering to the robber's(perpetrator's) in my life and after making it out alive, I saw no need to look back. Therefore, with much prayer and trust in God, I bounced back from my trauma and I knew I would live a much more meaningful life because of it. Just because I made it out did not mean I didn't have times when I would suffer with the pain of what I went through. My hands were no longer tied behind my back and the shackles were loosened from my ankles, but that didn't take away the experiences that changed my life. There was still much needed work to be done, however I still survived and thrived through the trauma and I was not going to stay a prisoner of my past. It was time to become visible and seen instead of staying invisible and hidden.

The Moment That Changed It All

One day in late June of 2004, I was minding my own business, not ever thinking later that evening was going to change my life. You don't usually go out looking for love you just so happen to be found by it at the right time. Although, I hoped for this magical moment of having the love of my life one day, I stopped looking after my marriage fell apart. It took me a while to believe someone could love me after what I went through. I no longer saw myself as damaged goods, but trusting again felt terrifying. Previously, I thought I needed to have someone to take up the empty space left by the absence of my father, that was true now. I just needed trust to feel safe and love to be even safer.

I was still on the fence about love and relationships, yet hopeful. I had been at some of the lowest places of my life when it came to love. I had little to no sense of what I was going to do with my love life, I wanted to put that on hold. I was not interested in dating or being in any kind of relationship with anybody other than my children, God, and myself.

I realized that late summer night that I really had a deep desire to be loved and I was so very deserving of it. Why was I even having those thoughts of love? As I discovered more about myself that night, I followed a rather unusual path, one I had never taken before. This was most definitely different than anything I could have ever imagined! I had been invited to an event that I later changed my mind about going to. When I did not arrive as expected, a friend who was in attendance called me and convinced me to come, so I eventually showed up. When I got to the event, there she was sitting at the dining room table eating crabs. I was not looking for someone that night, *where did she come from?*

The evening felt good, but strange. It was hot, but cool, the breeze was blowing, but time stood still… but not long enough. As the night was near its end I did not want to leave Her presence. It was something about the way she made me feel during the conversation and I did not want to lose that moment. There it was, my heart had aligned with a stranger and I did not feel afraid of wanting to let Her have it. This was so different, mysterious and unable to be put into words that made sense. I knew I had to tell Her how I felt, but how could I, she was a reflection of me—a woman. The connection was there, I hoped she felt it too, what if it didn't exist for Her. I could not simply just say, "You feel like my soul mate."

I could not trust myself with that truth. What if it was not real? But I felt it. Those words were hidden in my heart, I knew they could not stay there she had to know. I was not looking for Her; I did not even want to be in that space of availability. If she left, I would miss the opportunity of Her ever knowing how I felt. She is going to think I am crazy and just like that I let Her drive away only saying a few meaningless words and goodnight. I had to safely tuck away those feeling. *How was it even possible that I had that type of emotion about someone I did not even know?*

The next morning, I woke up still feeling the exact same way as the night before, so I was not dreaming. I knew it was possible for me to find a way to talk to Her, I just needed time to think. We might not always know our life's purpose, but I was glad I did not have to walk it alone. I was able to get Her number. I called, we spoke, and we laughed. We shared that we both felt the same way—an indescribable connection that neither one of us wanted to end! I was not alone last night in my feelings or what was in my heart… she felt it too! It was weird for the both of us we were strangers in the world, but we knew one another in our heart.

I was not ready for love; but it unexpectedly happened. I did not know if I could trust love because it had been so disappointing for me. After days, weeks, and months of talking to Her, she made me believe in her love for me. As the months passed, she told me countless times that I was the one for her and the searched ended the night she laid eyes on me. She was gentle and understanding of the pain of losing my parents, my unhealthy and toxic relationships, and how messy my overall life had been and yet there was no place she'd rather be. She actually listened and heard my cries, wiping my tears softly with her hands. This love was protective and unique it made me trust and believe in it, it felt safe.

She was ever so present, loyal, and consistent. She absolutely adored me. Her love was compassionate, beautiful and in its most natural form. She did not want to exist without being able to love me. She only wanted to live and breathe with me. She healed the broken parts of me with her patience and love. Her desire was to share space with me in the world and in my heart. She knew the trauma and everything I had been through but saw me as one in a million. She noticed my flaws, scars, wounds, imperfections and she wanted to be closer. It made me think for a minute. I wanted to find something wrong with Her, *why did she love me like this?*

I didn't want to reflect on my past love and all the mistakes I made, this was different, and I didn't want to scare Her away. She made promises to take care of me for the rest of my life, no one has ever said that to me and every promise that had been made from others had been broken. I pinched myself many times, because this could not be real, this is a fairytale only seen on television not experienced in real life. She had given me a purpose to smile, breathe, relax, trust, and to love. She taught me how to be fearless, free, and open with my heart to be loved without reservation. She knew it wasn't going to be easy loving me, but she had the blueprint to love and to my heart. I felt sorry for Her sometimes because I was difficult and struggled with love, but I knew she was the one; everything proved it. She always stayed near, never too far from my reach. She understood me and reminded me often that I was much more beautiful than my ugly past. She had a way with me like no one has ever had before. It was a strong emotional connection, one that could not easily be broken. My many years of hurt, pain, and trauma were real, but she smoothed it over like soft butter on bread and I was officially in love.

"Do one thing every day that scares you. Let that thing be love."
—Eleanor Roosevelt

Love Over Everything

When I showed up at that event I did not have a clue that I would meet my now spouse, life partner, best friend, and the current love of my life. We have five children, two grandchildren, and 17 years of a wonderful life full of ups and downs. She was breathtaking then and even more now for staying with me all of these years later. She kept her promises to me, something no one had ever done before. I still can't believe she chooses to love me more and more every day. She made me have a clear vision on love and now I not only see it, but I am experiencing it every day. She is everything sweet love is and supposed to be and poured every ounce of love she had in me. She changed my life for the better in every way. She encouraged, motivated, uplifted, and inspired me to be my best self and when we met I was not so certain who that actually was. She accepted every part of me and because of it I learned how to love in ways I never thought I could.

She was my shoulder to cry on as I was hers and we walked through this thing called life closely knitted together with all the pressures that came our way. Being a single mom and raising three boys was not something I had to keep doing alone. One of the best parts of Her was how she not only loved me, but my sons. I loved Her in an unexplainable way because of how she unconditionally loved them and for that she was admired all the more. When your children are loved right by the person who loves you, you in return love that person deeply. Some people come into your life for many reasons and she came into our life to stay and we welcomed Her.

Imagine being loved and thinking it couldn't get any better, well for me it did. She knew my dreams, I shared them with Her and she believed in them when I gave up. There were nights we would stay up talking about all the things I wanted to accomplish, all the places I only daydreamed about going, and every prayer I believed God would one day answer. For example, I wanted to go back to school, but I thought I was too old, and I put it off for many years. She told me age was not a factor and she pushed me into registering for college and I now have a master's degree in social work.

In addition, I am a published author, an inspirational and motivational speaker, and the founder of a group called Women of Truth, which inspires women from all walks of life to be true to themselves. She constantly showed me how right she was for my children and me. I would regularly have talks with myself like I was talking to someone as a reminder not to reject or questioned love because it was different. When I would have those self-talks, it helped me to close my eyes, breathe, and enjoy being loved.

I chose to be with Her and she loved me with good intentions and it felt right. We have traveled the world and I have been to places I had only dreamed of. She has taken me to islands in other countries with waters so clear I could see my feet in the water. I have sat at the finest restaurants where you wanted to put on your best dress, high heeled shoes, and order a nice crisp glass of wine with dinner. I was being swept off of my feet! This didn't mean there were no arguments, or things wasn't at times complicated, however, we enjoyed each other's company and knew life was going to be faced together and not apart.

My heart told me everything I needed to know about Her. She was different from any person I'd been in a relationship with before and not just because of the obvious. She was warm-hearted and catering to all of my emotional, mental, spiritual, financial, and physical needs. Every area of my life was fulfilled, happy, and satisfied. I did not plan for my life to go a specific way, but what I did plan for was one day finding my one true love. We share love because I finally had love to share with someone as deserving as Her and we are committed to a lifetime together. *She's the best thing that has ever happened to me and is the right person for me!*

"The best and most beautiful things in the world cannot be seen or even touched. They must be felt with the heart."
—Helen Keller

After the difficult and challenging obstacles I faced and loosing touch with myself, I was able to enjoy the simple things in life. Some of the many things I have learned were how to be strong, courageous, and resilient while listening to my inner self. Life experiences have been the best teacher with all of its ups and downs. And through it I was taught how not to play pretend as I usually did. I was not always true to myself or to those around me, which had me be out of alignment with myself. Letting go and hearing my own voice helped me realize what I truly wanted for myself and that was to be loved in the most patient way possible. A way that has brought me this far in life and where I am able from deep inside to feel what is true for me, the power of love.

She still makes me smile and my answer to Her is still "yes" and "I do!"

I stayed strong while being weak and stayed connected to God while my faith was being tested at every angle. We all have a story with different paths that we take, and mine was an example of how I SURVIVED my pain and my trauma and how I'm living my now truth.

Find someone who isn't afraid to admit that they miss you. Someone who knows that you are not perfect but treats you as if you are. Someone who's biggest fear is losing you. One who gives their heart completely. Someone who says, "I love you" and means it. Last but not least, find someone who wouldn't mind waking up with you in the morning seeing you in wrinkles and your gray hair but still falls for you all over again.
—Christina Slater

A Thank You Note

Dear Survivor,

Although parts of my life were uncomfortable, traumatizing and difficult to read, thank you for walking through this journey with me. It was one of the most gut-wrenching and traumatic experiences to relive as I shared my story with you. It was very challenging to tell my truth—it is never easy to dig up what you want to stay buried. I know child and adulthood trauma has long term effects that seem to never go away. We think by not talking about it somehow means it didn't happen and it will magically disappear, but it won't. It took me over forty years to talk about my sexual abuse publicly, it was shame and guilt that silenced me. In doing so, it caused me many years of trauma throughout my life and in relationships, even how I parented. It is important that you get what is inside of you out when you are ready to trust yourself and not care about the world's view of you. It is your story and you get to tell it however and whenever you want to.

If telling my truth can heal the physical wounds and emotional scars from mental and sexual abuse and give hope to one person, it was worth it. Life can be scary, especially when we don't have control over the hand that we are dealt. What you and I have been through in life broke us, but it did not destroy us. I am living proof that no matter how your story begins or all the things in between, how it ends is most important. Love yourself and the right person will love you too.

Now release the pain inside of you—you deserve to be free from it. It was never your fault, and you are not defined by your past. I say, "Live your life well; laugh until your belly hurts; and love with no regret."

There's a world full of endless possibilities that awaits you!

—*Monica Williams*

Me, my spouse, and our 5 children.

Speaking at college Millersville University.

Book signing January 2019.

My sons and my daughter.

My beautiful family.

All the children and our two grandchildren.

Me and Her.

Our twins born in 2012 and yes she carried the babies lol.

1st book photo shoot.

One of my greatest accomplishments.

Me at my Women's event about to speak.

They love their momma.

Me and my boys to men.

Graduated with my Masters Degree in Social Work May, 2016.

My first book.

Look how far we have come, I love these grown men!

God is so good, look at our children!

Me at my graduation in 2014, I received my Bachelor's of Arts Degree.

Graduated with honors Cum Laude 2014.

My amazing family.

ABOUT THE AUTHOR

Monica Williams is the founder of a women's empowerment group established in 2014 called Women of Truth. She is a graduate of Millersville and Shippensburg University, where she received her Master of Social Work. Monica was inducted into the Theta Alpha Phi Alpha Honor Society and has a certificate for Graduating Students of Color. In addition, she earned a Leader's in Training Experience certificate of completion.

Monica and her current spouse share a twin girl and boy and have a total of five children from previous relationships, as well as two grandchildren. Monica is a motivational speaker and author whose first book, How I Loved GOD and Her, was featured in the York Dispatch newspaper. She and her spouse enjoy vacationing and spending time with family and friends.

Monica currently lives in York, Pennsylvania, with her spouse and children.

Contact Monica:

Instagram: wew_womenoftruth
Email: monica.williams0313@gmail.com
Website: www.womenoftruthco.com

THE UNVEILING

Made in the USA
Monee, IL
19 February 2022

4f137464-c719-4d43-9e2e-55cbcc161d7bR01